The Certainty in Uncertain Times

FROM BLIND FAITH TO CONFIDENT CONVICTION

Debra L. Peters

Print ISBN: 978-1-4866-2367-9
eBook ISBN: 978-1-4866-2368-6

Word Alive Press
119 De Baets Street, Winnipeg, MB R2J 3R9
www.wordalivepress.ca

WORD ALIVE
—P R E S S—

Cataloguing in Publication may be obtained through Library and Archives Canada

This book is dedicated to my husband, T.J.,

my encourager and friend.

CONTENTS

ACKNOWLEDGEMENTS

There always seems to be a boatload of people to thank for helping on any project, and it's no different when writing a book.

Endless hours and tireless days in front of the computer seem to extend longer when beautiful weather beckons to be outdoors. Time is exchanged to create something of value, and this project was no different. It will be a worthwhile endeavour if someone gains a deeper knowledge of Jesus. It is precisely for you that this book was written.

There are many people I'd like to thank. To my encouraging husband, who would sit in the basement with me, either reading or praying while I typed away—this has become a vision embedded in my mind. I could feel his prayers, and I could also feel his frustration when I hesitated and continued hesitating to publish. But here it is, and I thank him. You are my cheerleader and life partner.

I want to give a special bouquet of thanks to my graphic artist, Julia Van Norden from Bliss Design, who also helped with research. She filled in the gap between the older (me) and the younger (her) and this in-between world of ever-changing technology. I needed her and her expertise and could not have done this without her. Thank you, Julia!

I want to acknowledge the helpful staff at Word Alive Publishing—Crystal, Jen, Kerry, and others. Thank you for taking the time to answer my questions. Your patience and guidance are greatly appreciated.

I thank all my friends who read my original letter and encouraged me to explore the possibilities of publishing. Thank you to Debby

Petryk and her keen eye in catching things I missed. The support I've received through other friends has been life-giving as well. Thanks to Sandra Hugill, Brenda Horch, Brenda-Lee Summers, Pauline Rioux, Esther Bissel, Brenda Cooke, Donna Meikle, Merrilyn Irvine, Aretha Johnson, and Rachel MacKay. Your encouraging words helped push me through to the finish line.

A great big thank you to my three musketeers—Gloria Kirouac, Judy Masse, and Elaine Lyons—my spiritual swashbucklers who watched my back when I was too weak to hold my own sword! I hold each of you close to my heart.

To my son Kurtis—thank you for your feedback and suggestions. I love being your mom! To my other kiddos—I love being your mom too!

To Tim Arndt, who did not hesitate for a moment to give me access to his article. Thank you for your kindness. Tim, may you be blessed for your generous gift and awesome attitude!

I'd also like to thank Jimmy Evans for his knowledge and ministry at Tipping Point. Your material has stretched both my husband and myself, and we're grateful for your years of study. We get to enjoy the fruits of your labour and your mission for "His Kingdom, His power, and His glory."

To Dr. Grant Richison—I am so grateful to you. You have no idea how the life-giving messages you taught instilled foundational biblical principles that helped me stay grounded when my world was falling apart. Those precepts and principles, based on the Word of God, anchored and secured me to see me through the tough stuff!

Lastly, in memory of one of my previous pastors, the late Leon Fontaine of Springs Church in Winnipeg, Canada. Leon's teaching from the Word would come into my heart and mind to create a fortitude and perseverance that helped me withstand the buffeting during the hardships of life. When listening to his teachings, I quickly realized that I didn't listen to his CDs until I was done with them, but instead I continued to listen until they were done with me! His teachings are woven throughout this book. Pastor Leon, you didn't shift your eyes to the left or the right but kept them solely focused of Jesus and His mission for your life. Because of this, you have my greatest respect, admiration, and gratitude. Your life mission of serving Him was evident in your (and your wife, Sally's) love for people, the country of Canada, and the body of Christ worldwide. You were a true example of a Christ-follower. You will be greatly missed, but the best is yet to come! We will meet again.

INTRODUCTION

The writer was emphatic about "introductions" and their purpose in a book. He explained that people don't want to read about one's self-serving attitude—they skip it and go to chapter one. Although I agree with him (as I usually skip it and go to chapter one), I wrote this portion for those who desire to read my introduction. I want to include you in knowing the purpose for my writing *The Certainty in Uncertain Times*. As I stalled and battled within myself, I guarantee that, from my perspective, there was nothing "self-serving" about this project. I reasoned why I couldn't and why I shouldn't, and I still felt compelled to write it. Whether it's written correctly remains to be seen. From what I've read, I already know I've got "lop-sided" chapters! However, my goal was never to have a perfectly written book but a book that would translate to the reader. There is a God who cares and loves each of us individually, intimately, and personally. When you seek Him, He is more than willing to be found.

This book began as a letter to my friends and family in April of 2020. I wrote the letter out of a reassurance I'd found during troublesome times in my life, and I aspired to pass that hope on to others. In times of isolation due to COVID-19, depression, mental anguish, and illness have spiked significantly. Those who were once secure in many aspects of their lives have found that the solid ground they once stood on is now shaken up and unsteady. During heavy periods of reflection, I made a personal commitment to soar upwards instead of spiraling downward—to go further, dig deeper, and draw closer to God.

The reflection was worth it. When we are willing to draw closer to the Father, we can nestle in and begin to hear His heartbeat. Time and commitments often stop us from hearing His heartbeat, but with more time and fewer commitments, I had no excuse. So I rewrote the letter, and as time passed, the letter evolved into a book.

On my travels, I began with questions that caused me to search. In that quest, God deposited many answers along the way, and I felt it was because I was making the effort to take the time to seek—like little gifts given to me just because I was on the road, questioning and hungering to get some answers from the One above.

My desire is that this piece of literature gives everyone who reads it a feeling of a little gift, a deposit from God, much like He gave me. I hope that you gain a deeper and broader understanding of the evidence of Jesus Christ, who He is, and the role He has to play in supporting us in times of crisis.

During times of personal pain, I pondered my life experiences and then wrote about how my faith became grounded and rooted through times of uncertainty. It all came down to one truth: there is *hope*. We all journey through periods of shadows and overcast skies that hover and cloud over each of us, and amidst COVID, many feel like they have lost hope completely, or have little to none left. Things aren't easy when we feel overwhelmed, but there is Someone who promises never to leave you or forsake you. You are not alone. Even when the world screams that you are, you can know that you have Someone at your side to see you through it all.

As I began writing this book, I added scripture from a specific version of the Bible. In recent years I've noticed a new trend: the more contemporary renditions of the Bible, as well as many Christian books, no longer capitalize the pronouns of God. This is a more current way of writing and is done for a variety of reasons. However, the more scripture I typed out in the modern style of my original choice of Bible selection, the more I became aware that this was not the right fit for me. So I decided to use the New American Standard

Bible (NASB) out of my personal preference and as my way of honouring God.

Throughout this book, I have consistently capitalized the pronouns of God. It's not a mistake and doesn't indicate that others who write differently are less reverent. This is a personal choice, and as I quote other authors and different Bible sources, you'll notice that they don't capitalize the pronouns. Personally, I am compelled to write God's titles with the first letter capitalized as my form of reverence, and I wanted to fill you in on the "why."

I have sought the Lord on this project, and there may be errors that my human nature transports, but my sincere hope is that it points others to the Light of the world. Any inspiration and direction I have succeeded in giving others is not of me but the One I seek after. As you read this book, my sincere prayer is two-fold: for those who already know Jesus, may this book strengthen your faith with solid bricks of the foundational truths from the Bible, and also the outside sources confirming those truths. For those who spiritually seek answers, may you discover the goodness and love of a benevolent and gracious God who offers you eternal life through Jesus Christ. At the end of your journey, may you find more than enough evidence to call Jesus your Saviour and Lord.

Part One

THE BACKGROUND

Chapter One

RECOGNITION
NEEDS KNOWLEDGE

Have you ever stumbled across someone and had the wrong perception of that person based solely on their appearance? I certainly have. I knew a wealthy man who wore shoes with holes in them and a sweater with worn-out elbows. His son was a friend to my then-boyfriend. We were invited for a visit to their "mini- resort" snuggled in the serene and beautiful Lake of the Woods, Canada. The cabin was magnificent, and the view of the lake drew you to a place of serenity. The father parked his water plane by the boathouse that housed additional visitors' quarters on the rooftop. I had heard of but never experienced the lifestyles of the rich and famous. What an incredible sight!

He was a wise businessman, and he was also at the cottage that weekend. When I looked at this man, I thought that no one would ever recognize him as a multi-millionaire. Beat-up clothing and foot-wear full of holes are not typically how I envision someone of wealth. After chatting a bit, I quickly discovered that these long-time pieces of clothing reminded this gentleman of his humble beginnings, of who he was and where he came from. They felt like comfort and home to him and always brought him back to who he truly was at heart. His wisdom extended beyond business!

This memory reminded me of a story I once heard about C.S. Lewis, the author of the Narnia Chronicles and many other pieces of literature. One of his new students mistook the Oxford don for the campus gardener. At that moment, he wasn't recognized as the wizard of words that had earned him many accolades, simply because of his appearance. After a quick conversation, this young student soon discovered who he was. It was evident that the "don of literature" did not "don" the appearance of what the student felt a professor should look like.

Perception

Our perception is a funny thing because it comes packed with a skewed view of ... well, our perception. That is, until we become equipped with knowledge. All things change once we know a person's background and history. Knowing who they were, where they came from, and the events and facts behind an individual helps to give us a balanced and more rounded picture of the person standing before us.

There was a certain figure in history whom many people didn't recognize. Perhaps it was because of His humility and *lack* of physical attractiveness. Isaiah 53:2 gives us an account: "*He has no stately form or majesty that we would look at Him, nor an appearance that we would take pleasure in Him.*" Because of this, many did not or chose not to recognize Him. It remains so today. However, by knowing the history and precision-fulfilled prophecies behind this individual, one will recognize the greatness hidden under the cloak of humility.

Jesus Christ came approximately two thousand years ago on His first visit (first advent) to earth. He is described as the Lamb of God who takes away the sins of the world (John 1:29). He entered the world for the first time to humbly serve as a suffering Servant (Isaiah 53) for all humanity. However, He promises to come back as a Lion (Revelation 5:5), a majestic Lion who will reign as King of all kings (Isaiah 9:6) and Lord of lords when He returns a second time (second advent) to this messed-up earth.

Taking the time to gather information and evidence about the history and the prophecies Jesus fulfilled can help one attain a fuller picture of who Jesus was and is. Similarly, when one doesn't take the time to gain knowledge of His background, they can't fully recognize who He is, nor can they fully comprehend the impact and difference He can make in our uncertain world and our individual lives. *He is the certainty in uncertain times.*

All things change once we know a person's background and history.

Chapter Two

CONFIDENCE IS
WHAT WE NEED

In the year 2020, people in our Western culture began turning on each other for taking the last package of toilet paper in grocery stores. Who would have thought we would come to this? There wasn't even a shortage of food or water! Hating ourselves, others, and God are common thoughts in unpredictable times. Those already dealing with mental health issues can feel like this is all too much. Hold tight—there are answers.

Fear

Fear is being expressed everywhere, and some of us are overwhelmed with anxiety. If we look at ourselves and others, we can become highly fearful, and it can overtake us. Don't let it! Get productive and don't indulge in a passive mindset. During times of uncertainty, when we're unable to do what we want, it might be helpful to ask ourselves: What do I do well? What can I do with the abilities I have been given? How can I help myself and others during times of isolation or loneliness? When we help others, it gets us outside of ourselves, and sometimes that's a good and needed place to be

Fear can become aggressive and turn into anger. If you're angry, I get it! We all get outraged at circumstances in our lives. I've been there, you've been there, and we've all bought the t-shirt and worn it! Anger is a human emotion that can evolve into something better if we choose to let it. Fear can become the catalyst to asking important questions and getting some answers. Then it can be harnessed and catapulted in the right direction.

We need to grieve, mourn, and process in order to heal, and anger is part of that process. But that same anger can propel us in search of something other than ourselves and a purpose outside of "me." A far greater design is ahead of you, and it's not about fulfilling all your wants and desires, simply because it was never meant to.

Hope

In times of uncertainty, we all look for hope. There is hope, and I'm only one of many who can attest to the fact that God pulled through when I cried out to Him. That doesn't mean that pain or suffering won't happen, but we have the One who knows the roads perfectly and can straighten, strengthen, and get us through the rugged patches in our lives. I've gone through very deep valleys (and if you've lived long enough, you have as well) and was able to navigate the curved and darkened paths because of God's role in my life. He proved Himself faithful.

Here's the thing, though—but a very big thing indeed: I had to do my part. It's not a one-way relationship; a faithful relationship always involves two participating individuals. Both have a role to play.

This hope I found through the darkest moments of life is not a popular viewpoint in our self-serving society. Real and true hope points to Someone bigger than us and outside of ourselves. The One who holds all the answers still answers today. I don't pretend to know all the answers, but I personally know the Someone who does.

Those of you who know Him, or will choose to know Him in the future, will have a power and a force behind you that will give you the strength and fortitude to propel you through your present crisis and things to come. You may choose to throw this reasoning away before you go much further, but here is the challenge: a fair chance will only become a fair chance when it's given a fair chance. Reading this piece may be the challenge you need to probe deeper and go further than yourself.

Can hope be found within ourselves when our whole world turns upside down and the globe's focus experiences a massive paradigm shift? When we aren't in control, are there answers? If you desire to feel hope again, you can find it. Ecclesiastes 3:11a states, *"He has made everything appropriate in its time. He has also set eternity in their heart …"* This verse tells us why we can't find satisfaction from anything else on the face of this planet—simply because we were never meant to. We were never meant to find confidence in anything less than an eternal relationship with God.

If unexpected and unwarranted change arrives on our doorstep, we can't simply ignore the signs of the times or hope it all goes away. When the ostrich buries his head in the sand, only one big body part sticks up and out, and it becomes target practice! Problems don't disappear because we wish them to. Don't stick your head in the sand. Target practice is painful!

Here's the thing, though—but a very big thing indeed: I had to do my part. It's not a one-way relationship; a faithful relationship always involves two participating individuals. Both have a role to play.

Confidence

If we look toward God, He promises to be by our side, no matter what.

The psalmist said it best when he spoke of God's intimate love for each of us. As His creation, we are uniquely made and have a Father who cares.

Lord, You have searched me and known me.
You know when I sit down and when I get up;
You understand my thought from far away.
You scrutinize my path and my lying down,
and are acquainted with all my ways.

Even before there is a word on my tongue,
behold, Lord, You know it all.
You have encircled me behind and in front,
and placed Your hand upon me.
Such knowledge is too wonderful for me;
it is too high, I cannot comprehend it.

Where can I go from Your Spirit?
Or where can I flee from Your presence?
If I ascend to heaven, You are there;
if I make my bed in Sheol, behold, You are there.
If I take up the wings of the dawn,
if I dwell in the remotest part of the sea,
even there Your hand will lead me,
and Your right hand will lay hold of me.
If I say, "Surely the darkness will overwhelm me,
and the light around me will be night,"
even darkness is not dark to You,
and the night is as bright as the day.
Darkness and light are alike to You.

For You created my innermost parts;
You wove me in my mother's womb.
I will give thanks to You, because I am awesomely and
      wonderfully made;
wonderful are Your works,
and my soul knows it very well.
My frame was not hidden from You
when I was made in secret,
and skillfully formed in the depths of the earth;
Your eyes have seen my formless substance;
and in Your book were written
all the days that were ordained for me,
when as yet there was not one of them.

How precious also are Your thoughts for me, O God!
How vast is the sum of them!
Were I to count them, they would outnumber the sand.
When I awake, I am still with you.

—Psalm 139:1–18

He knew you in the womb. He formed you, and He created you. He will see you through the rough times, and His light will make a way in the darkened paths of your life. It is promised for those who trust in Him, right here in Psalm 139.

Chapter Three

WE HAVE QUESTIONS.
ARE THERE ANSWERS?

In times of personal catastrophe, or something as big as COVID, we all have looming questions: When am I going to die? How am I going to die? But perhaps the better question is: Am I prepared to die? We prepare for life and retirement, so why do we put off preparing for death? Or worse yet, we don't think about eternity at all. It's simply too unpleasant and gives us an uneasy feeling. When we get that uneasy feeling, do we pretend it doesn't exist and ignore it, or do we dig a bit deeper? We will all reach the doorstep of eternity at one point in time. There is no escape hatch.

Investigating

Investigating the possibilities of life after death doesn't have to be frightening. When you gain understanding and knowledge to some of your questions, there can come a state of reassurance and peace that can ultimately draw you to the love of God. He desires for you to draw close to Him, and once you do, He can blanket you with His peace. That doesn't mean that the circumstances will change, but it does mean that you can give it to Him and let Him take control.

I've heard it said that in one aspect, nothing has changed in our world: "Yesterday I had no control, and God had all control; today I have no control, and God has all control." We all want control over our little world. But when our world stops and takes a breath, do we recognize Who's really in control? When all our idolized sports teams halt their games in a heartbeat, when our worshipped movie stars contract a disease they have no control over, when one can no longer chant at rock concerts, and when social events are closed, who do we choose to worship, idolize, and rock for then? Do we look inward and then upward, or do we continue to look outward to others for rescue?

A strong vertical relationship with the Almighty will also help us with our horizontal relationships. When we quiet our minds and souls long enough, when no distractions jostle for our attention, when we're locked up in the most surreal place of self-isolation, we may just begin to choose to look elsewhere than ourselves. And possibly, that may be the only way God can get some undivided attention.

There is a life-saver—His name is Jesus. We are made and called to worship, but our worship can be misplaced. Perhaps this is our time to explore the God of the universe and recognize and worship Him instead of things with temporal value, such as success, body image, fame, media, people, money, position, sports, power, work, and the list goes on. And just to bring clarity, God blesses us with good things. He is the Maker and the giver of all things good. None of the above-mentioned items are outside of God's realm of blessings. What matters is what we do with them. For example, money is not the root of all evil, but the love of it is (1 Timothy 6:10). When these things get in the way and distract us from our God-made focus—a relationship with Him—we can veer off course.

Has a human ever been able to spin the earth into orbit? Have you been able to rise and set the sun at your command? Do we take the time to thank our Creator for our provision, instead of expecting it to always be there for us? We have taken many things for granted—our food, health, healthcare system, friends, and family. Some things may not be here in the near future, including opportunities to worship. Things we never thought would disappear in our lifetime vanished in an instant. Simply put, we can worship the wrong things.

---

*When you gain understanding and knowledge
to some of your questions, there can come a
state of reassurance and peace that can
ultimately draw you to the love of God.*

Questions

I am a thinker and not a woman of faith. When pondering that thought, it really caught me by surprise. I realized how many questions I had and my need for answers—not only before placing my trust in Jesus, but afterward as well. As I reflected on this, I thought that if I could move into a position of faith intellectually, then maybe others who have struggled with faith could do so too. Perhaps others may need some answers to move from one place to another and ultimately into the knowledge and arms of a loving God.

I would label myself an average thinker, but others with great intellect and degrees behind their names also believe that Christ is the answer to humanity's troubles. You don't have to leave your brains at the door (as some seem to believe) to discover that true salvation for the entire world is available through the power of Jesus Christ and His death on the cross. It will just take a bit of excavating on your part to gain a greater understanding of the evidence that is readily at your fingertips. Both the modestly-educated and biblical scholars can discover solid explanations to the tough questions. Many intellects of the faith can answer your difficult questions, and the different authors I recommend in this book can answer most of them. Just as I have had mine answered, you can too.

I've heard that entering a barn doesn't make you a farmer, and entering a church doesn't make you a Christian. That is a statement worth pondering! Let me begin my story by saying that I entered my faith as a child in the Catholic Church. At a young age, my family attended mass regularly every Sunday. The church and the catechism classes helped to create a reverence for God within me and taught me about Jesus' birth and His death on the cross. But for me, that's where it ended. Repeated traditions and rituals spoken in either Latin or Ukrainian during the mass did nothing for my child-like mind, and my soul never knew of a God who wanted a personal relationship with me. As the years passed and my siblings and I became young teens, the world's distractions took over. Those were my B.C. days (meaning my "before Christ" days), and those distractions worked hard to win the tug-of-war. Today, battle scars remain from that war, and even though I'm forgiven, I regret the hurt I may have caused others.

Looking back, I recognize what caused the gap in my (as well as my family's) faith walk. There was little to no teaching from the Word of God or encouragement to read His Word. That created a huge chasm between God and His creation—me. I was totally unaware of this gaping hole, but I realize now that many others who are simply attending church have experienced this chasm as well. Knowing about His personal love for each of us can only begin to happen when we read the Bible for ourselves and understand what was done on our behalf. The bridge between the chasm of humanity and God is a personal relationship with Jesus.

There is no perfect church and no perfection outside of Heaven. That includes all churches and the people housed in them. Every church and every person in and out of it has "issues." My story of how I got to where I am today isn't about attending a certain church but about getting to know Jesus personally. We can attend church all our lives and still not know Jesus.

Without proper teaching backed by the Word of God, I fell in line with others who believed that God exists but that once He created us, He kind of threw us into the universe to fend for ourselves. With that mindset, I was spiritually lost. My faith was stunted and remained at a standstill. I believed in a God but not a God who cared or took a personal interest in any of His creation. Yet the reality is that nothing could be further from the truth. When you begin to read, study, and understand the Bible, it heralds the announcement of an amazing love, to the point of self-sacrifice *for* His creation.

My faith was halted for a period of time, but once I started attending high school, I began hanging out with a group of friends who were Christians. I liked them. They probed and got to know me and challenged me. Once in a while they would pepper me with spiritual questions, and I seasoned them back with tough ones as well. Some of them were answered, but some remained unanswered. However, one girl stood out from the crowd. Debbie Voth was a modest young lady with no striking appearance about her, but there was a force within her that made her so attractive that I desired to be around her. I enjoyed her company. I could sense that she had God's love within her, and I felt like she genuinely cared about me.

When I examined my thoughts, I realized that I felt invisible to the people in my world. However, I never felt that way with her. One day we were laughing over something silly. After the laughter, she turned to me and said the simplest yet most profound thing: "Debbie, God made someone real special when He made you." I was stunned. I didn't know God cared about me in the slightest way, never mind that He would think of me as special. Her words were exactly what I needed to hear when struggling with self-identity. I was at a loss for words but interested in what she knew about God. I craved that "something" she had that I didn't. She had a genuine perkiness that came from the inside out, and it was not complex. She simply extended love to others.

Many times she invited me to church, but I was being pulled in two different directions. I went with her once in a while but not consistently. If I came home late on a Saturday night, I'd immediately take the phone off the hook (there were no cell phones back then) so that it couldn't ring and I could get in some extra zzzs on those Sunday mornings. I went through the entirety of high school this way and she never reprimanded me. There were mornings when both she and her parents would wait for me outside my home to join them for church, but my phone was off the hook and I was sleeping soundly.

A tug-of-war was happening within me. One side wanted to know about God and Jesus more than ever before, and one desired to live my life my way. As far back as I can remember, I dreamed of becoming an "actress" (now the term is "actor"). Lacking self-identity and self-importance drew me into the world of acting where I could momentarily become someone else, and where I was seen and no longer invisible. I began taking lessons from a theatre school. It was the greatest paradox of my life. I was incredibly shy and timid, but not a soul there knew how introverted I was, so I pretended to be highly sociable instead. Looking around and confirming that there were no familiar faces, I continued my master charade. Soon those in my theatre class wanted me to be the leader in their group. I began taking acting lessons at around thirteen years old, before high school, and a new me began to emerge. The world of theatre drew me out of myself, and I began to find my creative niche. By the time I reached high school, the new me surfaced and I was able to be outgoing around others, but inside there were internal battles.

I had a great imagination and could become many characters. I dreamed of being an actor on Broadway. It was a very real dream, and I started planning how to make that happen. However, God's plan was greater. It's interesting how God works in the lives of people and makes Himself known in small (and sometimes large) ways. God used the creative arts to reach me. Who would have thought it? So here's the goods—and don't shoot the messenger (that would be me). Before I go further, remember that God can use all things for His good purposes (Romans 8:28), even though the situation or persons involved may not be ideal. My story goes like this. Two film versions of musicals about who Jesus claimed to be intrigued me: *Godspell* and *Jesus Christ Superstar*. Today I understand that some of the lyrics aren't God-honouring, but these musicals were definitely used at that time in my search and my desire to know more about Jesus. I came out of the movie theatre desiring to read the Bible and wanting to get to know Jesus in the way the Bible spoke of Him, and not how the movies portrayed Him. I began reading it on my own with no persuasion from anyone else.

I steadily continued with theatre lessons, which combined drama, vocal coaching, singing, and choreography. Then it wasn't long before I began working in the industry with bit parts in local movies, TV commercials/programs, and voice over work. I was now privy to step behind the glitz and glitter of the shimmering curtain, but the glamour quickly dissipated. It didn't take long to recognize that it wasn't pretty back there. In fact, it was very messy. Behind the veil of the hype, I saw a world that greatly clashed with my morality. I was confused because I loved the creative arts and had such a desire to pursue my dream. I saw how far others went and what they were willing to do to reach for the stars. I wasn't so sure I liked this bill of goods that seemed to come as a package deal. The word "compromise" was clearly stamped in the middle of that bill of goods.

There was that private war again, and I had to make a decision. After auditioning for a TV movie in which the character used the Lord's name in vain, I saw clearly what I needed to do. I refused the part. Then I spent some serious time evaluating and deeply weighing my options. I made a decision to surrender my dream of being an actor and took a step of faith to begin trusting God. I simply wasn't willing to give up "me" for "it." That was the second-wisest choice I ever made. I chose to make a decision to accept Jesus into my life and heart (that was the wisest choice). It was a blind step of faith, and I didn't have all the answers, but I knew that I couldn't live in that world and be honouring to God, so I closed the backstage door completely and left it all behind. I chose to trust that He had the best plan for me, and in hindsight, I see that He did. He gave me my heart's desires. It was never about being famous or successful but being known and belonging. I had that the moment I accepted Jesus. Ultimately we all search for the same thing—to be known and to belong; we just achieve it through different means.

In the jungle of that industry, a person better know who they are, where they are going, and how they're going to get there. They need to decide beforehand what they will and will not compromise. Success can swallow you whole if you're not prepared for it, no matter what profession you're in. We don't have to look far for examples in the arts and entertainment world. How many simply self-destruct? The ones who seemingly have it all? There can be emptiness once we reach the pinnacle of success. It's possible to have "everything" yet have nothing (Mark 8:36). Success is neither good nor bad, but it needs to be channelled to take us where we want to go.

Today there is a new world of Christian movies, writers, producers, and actors. How exciting! You can pray on the set and honour God with your talents! Without any foresight on my part, God gave drama and the creative arts back to me in a way I never would have thought possible. As I grew into young adulthood, and with the creative training I had tucked away in my back pocket, I would begin to see God use it in my future. Through various Christian avenues, I began acting, directing, writing, and teaching drama. However, it was different—completely different—because it was for His purposes and ministry. I now had control over my choices and would shoot the odd TV commercial or bit part without compromising who I was. I realize that it was small-town-peanut kind of stuff compared to Hollywood, but it fulfilled the longings of my original dream. When I accepted Jesus, I gave it all to Him, and He returned the arts back to me. I was amazed when I saw Him begin to use the passion within me. I was able to pull it out of my back pocket and say, "This belongs to You; use it as You see fit." I think you can agree that sometimes it's a good thing that God doesn't answer all our prayers the way we want Him to.

I found the security I longed for—not in fame or being known, but in having a loving relationship with God. In hindsight, I am so glad that God chose my path for me, because He had the best in mind. At such a young age, I wasn't ready or prepared to make wise choices—I was so busy chasing a dream that I forgot to look back at the cost! Throughout my life, I have endlessly thanked Him for not fulfilling that dream. And I've been able to use the creative arts in different formats. One of them is this book.

As a new Christian, my questions about Jesus and the Bible never stopped coming, and I would write them down. On Sunday mornings, I'd wave a pastor down to probe him for answers (actually, come to think of it, I still do). I'm sure some of them went running when they saw me approaching.

I'm the curious sort, constantly processing, both then and now. I began buying books on the toughest questions about my new-found faith, and I got answers to a myriad of questions. The drawstrings drew closer to align my faith with my challenging internal debate. This curiosity drove me to readily available answers, but it required making the time and doing some digging to gain the obtainable knowledge. I thought that if eternity was the real deal, as God said it was, then the archeological dig would be worth the effort!

In later life, I had more questions, some prompted by the blackness of depression. Dark hours, days, years, or decades have clouded over each of us. Infidelity in my first marriage caused the deepest pain I could have possibly imagined. The times of greatest depression allowed me to cry out to God in my anger. He knew my thoughts anyway, so I wasn't hiding the rage that was evident in my waking hours. His shoulders were big enough to take it. I sought Him during this time instead of running away from Him. James 4:8 invites us to *"Draw near to God, and He will draw near to you"* (NKJV). If we look carefully at this verse, we'll realize that this is an invitation, not a forced entry. So I did. I drew near to Him, and through the fear and trembling of each new day, I asked Him to hold my hand so we could do life together. It's been a journey filled with doubts and questions but also one in which He proved Himself faithful. That trauma has now become my testimony. I know that if He saw me through my anguish, He'll see you through yours.

God gave each of us different abilities, and He can use my abilities to reach those of you who want to hear and who may have the same type of struggles and questions that I wrestled with. I hope you'll stick around for some answers.

Chapter Four

LET'S START
WITH THE BASICS

I want to present you with some evidence pointing to the Christian faith's reliability, because that information pulled the drawstrings together for me. It aligned answers to my questions that strengthened my faith. The more resolve I received, the closer the drawstrings met, and the narrower the gap became.

Is this just my truth? You can say that if you believe in moral relativity (your truth is your truth, and mine is mine, because there are no moral absolutes). However, I desire to go beyond that; God stated that this truth was the hope for all humankind (John 3:16). It's not a made-up truth I'm trying to convince you of but a tangible piece of history, with solid facts backed up by data, eyewitness accounts, and historical documentation. If you're like me and have many questions, hopefully some of them will be answered. This will help to bring clarity to biblical future events as well. This truth that has become mine isn't just true for me but for whoever wants to receive it throughout the entire world. As the evidence grew, so did my faith.

Begin with This Premise

There are nice and smart Christians, and there are also nice and smart non-believers in Christ. Both have smart people on their side of the fence. It's not a lopsided teeter-totter, with the intellectual non-believers weighing down one side of the seesaw. There are a balanced number of intellectuals on the field.

Some people think that Christians decide to believe based on a childlike faith, or that Christians are simple-minded people, an assumption based on a lack of knowledge. Many of us have dug deep to attain answers before accepting Jesus, and many have wrestled with the tough questions of Christianity before standing up and taking their stance in the faith. Although our belief can begin with the faith of a child, it's not always so; mine began that way, but it didn't stay that way. Many intelligent people have struggled with the big questions before coming to a conviction of who Jesus is.

J.R.R. Tolkien (*Lord of the Rings*) used his intellect to lead C.S. Lewis (*Chronicles of Narnia*) to a knowledge of and then faith in Jesus. Other agnostics and atheists, such as Lee Strobel, Josh McDowell, and J. Warner Wallace, are intellectuals who went on a journey to disprove the Christian faith. As they gathered evidence along the way (some on a two-year search), they accepted Christ as Lord and Saviour. These authors—some journalists, would-be lawyers, and forensic specialists—took the long, rugged path of asking the questions and doing the research. They went on a research mission to disprove Jesus' claims, but their search took them on a different pathway, and certainly one they didn't anticipate. The answers they discovered are also available to you. They have already spent the time and resources to journey out and study the evidence. Look online at any of these authors for answers to the tough questions. They have already done the archeological work for you. They did the digging, and you reap the benefits!

Lee Strobel's books, *The Case for Faith* and *The Case for Christ* (the latter was made into a movie), wrestle with the biggest and most challenging questions about life and the Christian faith. J. W. Wallace was a former atheist who used his skills as a homicide detective in interrogating and investigating the Christian faith. He began with the same questions he used to attack his homicide cases. Wallace explored Christianity and other world religions, packed with a suitcase full of probing inquiries. He examined the grounds to draw conclusive facts. The cross-examination provided enough evidence about who Christ claimed to be, and with that Wallace made an educated decision to follow Jesus. This spurred him to write *Forensic Faith, Cold-Case Christianity,* and *God's Crime Scene.*

Although one can't answer all spiritual questions this side of Heaven, many of them can be answered. God alone holds all the answers. These intellectuals were convinced by affirming facts they were confronted with, so it wasn't a simple act of faith. Their act of faith derived from the facts they encountered. The evidence they discovered, as well as their willingness to tear down their barricade of pride, moved them into this new position. You can come into faith very simply, or you can come struggling and sometimes even kicking, with intelligent questions in tow. It's okay to ask questions and to doubt, but there are also answers. Simply giving up and saying that you can't be bothered means it isn't important enough to you. If that's the case, you can't tear down the Christian faith with presumptions, especially with a lack of knowledge and a refusal to take the time to examine the evidence presented by authors like the ones suggested here.

During personal times of crisis, we can use the season to examine the evidence presented to strengthen ourselves in this faith instead of pondering on the uncertainty of our destinies and our eventual deaths. Whether through COVID or some other circumstance, we will all face the inevitable. Examining the evidence is worth the effort, even if it makes us uncomfortable to do so.

What about Those Who Have Never Heard?

God and eternity exist, whether we believe it or not. Their existence is not founded on our personal and sincere bents of beliefs. We can be sincere and be sincerely wrong. God provides revelation, knowledge, and evidence of Himself that He alone has lavishly presented to us. Romans 1:19–20 says:

> *Because that which is known about God is evident within them; for God made it evident to them. For since the creation of the world His invisible attributes, that is, His eternal power and divine nature,*

*have been clearly perceived, being understood by what has been
made, so that they are without excuse.*

People often ask about those who have never heard of the gospel
of Jesus. If people have not heard of Jesus, God makes Himself known
through nature (Romans 1:19–20) and other means, so no one has an
excuse for not believing in Him. I'm not sure how He will judge those
who have never heard the name of Jesus, either because they never
had the opportunity or were born before His coming to earth, but
God knows how to judge the hearts of humanity, and I'm glad that
responsibility is His alone.

God alone is Omnipresent, Omnipotent, and Omniscient—
everywhere present, all-powerful, and all-knowing. He is a righteous
Judge, so we know that He will be able to handle every individual with
justice and mercy. We can leave that to Him. God alone knows the
standard of measurement He will use, and this is best left in His hands.
Isaiah 45:5–6 says:

*I am the Lord, and there is no other; there is no God besides Me. I
will gird you, though you have not known Me, that they may know
from the rising of the sun to its setting that there is none besides Me.
I am the Lord, and there is no other.* (NKJV)

I like the part that states "... *they may know from the rising of the sun to
its setting that there is none besides Me.*" Nature announces that there is a
God, and God speaks to the entire world through His creation. I've
taken spectacular pictures of sunsets. We can see God's glory and mas-
terpiece artwork extend across the heavens by looking at His creative
attributes, such as the sun's rising and setting. With each sunset, His
fingertip flows onto the canvas of the sky. I see the magnificent blends
of purples, hues of blues, and bright pinks that burst into flamin-
go-orange flames. They blaze across the sky landscape, and I enjoy
His finger-painting at work! So do you. Nature is a testimony to God.
People naturally want to be close to the earth: to garden and plant,

camp, hike, feel the sunshine, enjoy beautiful waterfalls, and smell the fresh air. It brings us closer to God. His DNA imprint throughout nature and His glorious handiwork draw us near to Him.

Some may have never heard the name of Jesus, but many *have* heard about the message of Jesus. In Western society, we have every avenue available to us to hear about Jesus and His sacrifice. A good portion of people in the Western world say they believe in God. Even in the New Testament people thought that believing in God was enough, but it isn't. Why? Even the devil believes in God: "*You believe that God is one. You do well; the demons also believe, and shudder*" (James 2:19). It's not a matter of just knowing about God; it comes down to investigating who Jesus said He was and His substitutionary death on the cross for you. Then you must decide to accept or reject Him as Lord and Saviour of your life.

In his book *Heaven,* Randy Alcorn explains:

> In Heaven we'll see clearly that God revealed himself to each person and that he gave opportunity for each heart or conscience to seek and respond to him (Romans 1:18–2:16). Those who've heard the gospel have a greater opportunity to respond to Christ (Romans 10:13–17) … God is absolutely sovereign and doesn't desire any to die without Christ (1 Timothy 2:3–4; 2 Peter 3:19).[1]

He makes Himself known through the gospel, our conscience, and all of creation.

In Proverbs 8:17, the God who does not lie says to each of us, "*I love those who love me, and those who diligently seek me will find me.*" Some tribes may have never heard of the name of Jesus, but they can still be seekers of God. God knows the heart of every person who lived throughout history. He has made Himself known by demonstrating His powers in the sky, heavens, and nature. He is available, but this is a two-way relationship, and any quality two-way relationship requires both parties to work at it. Some people want God to magically appear to them, but He is the One who wrote the Instruction Manual, and He designed *you* to seek *Him*. When you do, He will be found.

God alone is Omnipresent, Omnipotent,
and Omniscient—everywhere present,
all-powerful, and all-knowing.

The Manual

You don't have to look far for this Instruction Manual. We use instruction manuals for many things in life, but we have one designed by our Manufacturer to guide us on life's road. When you want to know how your vehicle works, you grab the manual. God is our Manufacturer. He has fine-tuned us and given us specific directions and instructions to help us run our lives efficiently and to the best possible capacity. It's right in the Manual called the Bible.

This Manual will tell you about the upcoming bumps in the road that may cause you to get off course and the detours to take when you do. Plus, incredibly enough, the Manufacturer Himself promises to be right there beside you throughout your journey. He is the best roadside assistant, travelling with you to your final destination. This Manual is not a secret, and it's not hidden. It's within our reach and readily available—at least it is presently, on my side of the world, but I'm not sure that will always be the case.

I like this simple acronym:

B - Basic, **I** - Instructions, **B** - Before, **L** - Leaving, **E** - Earth. The Bible remains the bestseller of all time. However, it wasn't so accessible centuries back. Throughout history, all books were hand-printed, hence the job of scribes—to transcribe important people's statements or copy documents into legible and functional pieces of literature. It wasn't until the printing press became a reality that common folk (if they could afford to be educated) could even dream of holding a Bible, never mind reading it.

Personally, I love the simplicity of *The Message Bible*. However, others may not care for it. We are all unique. For those who may be starting on a journey of understanding the Word (Bible), I suggest *The Message Bible* for its clarity and simplicity. It helps me when I get stuck on verses or even chapters in other versions of the Bible. I also use commentaries and other aids when I want to dig deeper, but I seem to come back to *The Message*. Others may disagree, saying this or that Bible is the only way to go. But if a person hesitates to read scriptures daily because they're hung up on the wording, what good is that? We should look forward to reading it and not be apprehensive. The New Testament is a great place to start. It begins with the book of Matthew. First John tells us that Jesus is infinite and eternal, and many suggest to begin here.

The Message Bible can be used as a complementary companion to another style of Bible or as the primary reading source. I always come back to this version to gain clarity through simplicity. With my creative mind, I love verses that add a bit of sparkle to a word picture and capture my attention.

I came across Psalm 8:3–4 in *The Message* as I wrote this section:

> *I look up at your macro-skies, dark and enormous, your handmade sky-jewelry, moon and stars mounted in their settings. Then I look at my micro-self and wonder, Why do you bother with us? Why take a second look our way?*

Yet God desires a relationship with each of us. His fingerprint is everywhere. Daily Bible reading is the place to begin. If we truly want to find God, we will seek Him, and He will be there. If we do our part, He promises to do His. It is here where we begin the journey.

Chapter Five

MORAL AND
ETHICAL HISTORY

Jesus revolutionized the course of moral and ethical history. He did! So radical was He that He changed the dynamics of many cultures and beliefs. Jesus and His teaching took everyone by surprise, including the disciples and other Jesus followers. This extreme 180-turn threw many off the grid: the Jewish leaders, the Romans, the Gentiles, and even the followers themselves. What they thought was right-side-up became upside-down. New ideas and teachings and fresh thoughts provoked the world into a new and unprecedented way of living.

No wonder the religious leaders wanted to chase this man out of their synagogues! His teaching challenged their religion and culture. They wanted Him out of their region, out of their places of worship, and out of their lives! So for those of you who have a picture of Jesus as a long-haired, peace-loving, hippie-type-of-guy ... you've got the wrong dude!

The Radical

Christ didn't compromise when He was looked upon as a rebel, nor did He when being offensive to the religious leaders of the day. He told them, "*I am the way, and the truth, and the life; no one comes to the Father except through Me*" (John 14:6). That *is* a radical statement! He was a total revolutionary. He did the opposite of what people thought He should do, and He only did what the Father requested of Him.

His ideas were like oxymorons on steroids: the first will be last, and the last will be first; if you want to be a leader, you must be a servant; to really live, you must die to yourself. And those are just a few! He had upside-down and inside-out ideas. Never before were the Jewish religious leaders of the day challenged by such thinking, and with that line of thinking, they wanted Him out of the picture!

He loved and touched lepers when the world shouted, "Stay back!" He forgave individuals of their sins (which ultimately resulted in His death), implying that He was God. He raised the dead; He was a friend to all—including prostitutes and tax collectors (who were the dung of society). He healed people on the Sabbath day; He hung out with children and played with them, which was considered a huge no-no and a waste of His time when there was so much to do. Instead, Christ reprimanded the disciples by saying, *"Leave the children alone, and do not forbid them to come to Me; for the kingdom of heaven belongs to such as these"* (Matthew 19:14).

All of His creation is equal in His eyes, and Jesus hung out with the women as well as the men. When the day's culture regarded women as second-class citizens (and as we know, in some cultures they still do), Christ elevated them to a place of prominence. These faithful women were the first to see Him after His resurrection—not the male disciples, which points to the truth of the disciples' testimonies. They didn't fudge the report but instead ate humble pie when they recounted that the women were the first to see Jesus at the tomb and not themselves. They didn't make their stories seem larger than life. In a culture that didn't value the testimony of women, there was no room to embellish the story if they were being honest with their God. Men were the focal point of that day, not women, proving that their writings were true to the events.

Ways in Which Jesus Turned the World Upside-Down

The moral and ethical shifts Christ caused in His world, and even today (for those who choose to follow), are profound. That paradigm shift comes from a moral compass with moral guidelines made by a moral God with definite absolutes. There are "absolute" right and wrongs in this world, given by an absolute God with absolute guidelines. We don't have to doubt or make up our own absolutes. God has made them clear in His Word.

Tim Arndt wrote an excellent online article titled, "6 Undeniable Ways Jesus Changed the World for the Better." These are only a few ways that Jesus helped to unfold a new culture by changing the course of moral and ethical history. Although there are many others, let's touch on these. I've summarized Tim's main points below:

1. Women's Rights. Throughout history, there have been endless examples of women being mistreated. When Christianity arose about two thousand years ago, many called it a women's religion. Jesus made the difference. He treated women with dignity, respect, and a pure love that stood in stark contrast to society. Today, in un-Christianized parts of the world, discrimination toward women continues.

2. Human Rights. Today most Americans think that human rights are common sense and humanity should be treated with dignity and respect. But it wasn't always so. When Christianity began, so did emancipation. Today, many forces that fight for the freedom of others come from the Christian community. Caring for our fellow human stems from the teachings of Jesus.

3. Humanitarian Aid. Luke 14:13 shows us that caring for the poor and needy was always a part of Jesus' ministry. He cared for orphans, widows, and the helpless. He calls each of His followers to do the same. It's reported that 75% of US charitable organizations are faith-based.

4. Education. St. Patrick's ministry in Ireland began with literacy. In fact, most universities in England and America were started by Christians who promoted education. In the modern world, Christians have done more to inspire education in the modern world than any other group.

5. Science. Medieval Christians were the first to tie science and God together. For much of history, people thought of the world as being controlled by spirits or gods that influenced the forces of nature.

Many early scientists, such as Newton, saw their science as a means of uncovering traces of God's handiwork.

6. Changed Lives. Changed lives and people's personal testimonies reveal the hand of God transforming a person's heart, mind, and soul.[2]

Humanitarian Aid

Let's examine just one of the six ways that Tim Arndt describes how Jesus changed the world for the better—humanitarian aid. As he said, in the US, 75% of all humanitarian aid comes from the Christian community. Why is this? Because God calls us to in His Word. If we are suffering, we desire compassion. Compassion is an attribute of God, and one He wants us to extend to others. "*... love one another; just as I have loved you ... By this all people will know that you are My disciples: if you have love for one another*" (John 13:34–35).

Humanitarian aid is present worldwide and through many Christian organizations. After completing my work in a Christian non-government agency in Alberta, Canada, I requested something I'd been eyeing for months. They had some Bibles in stock that I had never seen before. They were produced by the Canadian Bible Society and called *the poverty and justice bible* (yep, lower case). On the back of the Bible, it reads:

> They all said it—poverty appears over 2,000 times in the Bible. So we went looking and highlighted almost 3,000 verses that show what the Bible says about poverty and justice. So you can see too—at a glance ... Now you can get the full picture on what God wants us to hear on one of the issues closest to His heart.[3]

Just reading that filled me with questions. What was I doing for the needy of the world? How could I make a difference in even one person's life? Highlighted in this Bible were all the verses about injustice, human suffering, and the aid God desires us to extend to others.

As Christians, we're called to be a conduit of His love. Why? Because this God of the Bible wants all nations to know Him personally and to know of His great love for each person individually. Are you poor, impoverished, sick, or suffering from addictions or mental illness? He loves you—this Jesus came for the suffering, the dying, and the lost. Endurance through the difficult times—and there will be difficult times—begins with knowing Jesus.

Extending humanitarian aid shows us and others God's heart and love for all. I recently read a book by Franklin Graham called *Living Beyond the Limits*. He describes the mission work he and others have undertaken in the most remote and destitute places on earth. The bravery of these people of missions astounds me! They sacrifice so much of themselves. Some have given their entire lives for the sake of others. This type of self-sacrificing completely blows me away! I'd love to say that I'd jump at this sort of opportunity, but it takes a person who is selfless, ruthless in their faith, and trusts God completely to take the most incredible mission-impossible-like risks. These are the true heroes of the faith! I am not there yet.

Franklin shares about a man he was caring for and ministering to. The man's words will stick with me forever: "You Christians are the only ones who help us."[4] Franklin shares other stories and states that these sentiments are often echoed throughout the land of missions. Let's examine this a bit. The reason why Christians help others is answered in the Bible—because God calls us to! In Matthew 22:37–39, we read:

> *Jesus said to him, "You shall love the Lord your God with all your heart, with all your soul, and with all your mind." This is the first and great commandment. And the second is like it: "You shall love your neighbor as yourself." On these two commandments hang all the Law and the Prophets.*

Humanitarian aid is just one of the profound ways Jesus changed the course of history. The Bible calls His people to care for others so we can point them to the love of God. Once those individuals know the power of Jesus' love for them, they can pass it on to others. It's the greatest recycling program going!

Historical Confirmation of Christ on Earth

Historians around the world have recognized that Christ walked the earth, whether they are believers or not. We have the early testimonies of the disciples, but other historians recognized the changes that transformed our world and culture through Jesus, and many of them were not followers. They can't deny that Jesus made differences in the then-known world that live on in many cultures today.

The nineteenth-century historian Philip Schaff gave us much insight when he said:

This Jesus of Nazareth;

without money and arms, conquered more millions than Alexander, Caesar, Mohammad, and Napoleon;

without science and learning, shed more light on things human and divine than all philosophers and scholars combined;

without the eloquence of schools, He spoke such words of life as were never spoken before or since and produced effects which lie beyond the reach of orator or poet;

without writing a single line, He set more pens in motion, and furnished themes for more sermons, works of art, and songs of praise than the whole army of great men of ancient and modern times.[5] (emphasis added)

Let's start with this—the evidence for the existence of Jesus is stronger than for any other ancient historical figure. Michael Green, an internationally renowned theologian from England, once stated:

If you're open to evidence at all, the evidence for the existence of Jesus ... is stronger than for any other ancient historical person. Much stronger, for instance, than for Julius Caesar. And you don't change the whole era of human history over a mythical figure. It happened over a historical person.[6]

From Josephus, the Jewish historian, to Tacitus, the Roman historian, to many eyewitnesses, Christ's birth, life, death, and resurrection have been well documented throughout history. Other historians (Lucian of Samosata, Suetonius, Pliny the Younger, Thalius, Phlegon, and more) have also provided historical documentation on Christ and the Christians that followed Him. And although these historians may question who Jesus claimed to be, they don't question His existence.

In his book *The New Evidence That Demands a Verdict*, Josh McDowell provides examples of these historians' writings and what each of them wrote about Jesus. For example, Cornelius Tacitus (AD 55–120) was a Roman historian who wrote about the Roman Empire between AD 14–68 (AD 68 being the time of Nero's death) in his book, *Annals*. He writes about the early Christians in book 15, chapter 44. The Roman Emperor Nero blamed the Christians for many things, including the Great Fire of Rome in AD 64. Even others could see the injustice that came from Nero's madness. This passage is one of the earliest written by an unbeliever about the Christian faith, confirming the death of Jesus Christ as well as a number of His followers. So those who quickly dismiss the historical evidence of Jesus need to rethink what they've been told, who told them, and why they accepted it as truth. If we do a bit of digging, the evidence is clear.

These historians recorded the events of their day without bias. Jewish historian Flavius Josephus wrote about Jesus of Nazareth, John the Baptist, and Jesus' brother James in *Antiquities of the Jews*. He recorded that Jesus "was called Christ." In book 18, chapter 5, he talks about the imprisonment and death of John the Baptist, and in book 20, chapter 9, he writes about James.

In *Antiquities*, it speaks of Nero's madness and viciousness. Martyrs of the Christian faith are mentioned as well, which could have included some of the five hundred witnesses that Paul wrote about in AD 56. In 1 Corinthians 15:3–8, Paul mentions that many of the witnesses were still alive (as it was a number of decades after Christ's ascension) to testify about seeing Jesus after the crucifixion. They saw a resurrected Jesus alive after His crucifixion and would *not* renounce their faith in the Christ at any cost. These new believers saw something that radically changed them from the inside out and caused a dramatic transformation, from being cowards to becoming martyrs. People have tried to argue that the witnesses who saw Christ after His resurrection were hallucinating, but incidents of hallucinations are unique to each individual. It's not possible that five hundred people could have had the *same* hallucination. These individuals were willing to stake their lives on what they saw and believed. The testimony of what they observed was consistent.

Novelist, teacher, journalist, and historian H. G. Wells said, "I am an historian, I am not a believer but I must confess as a historian that this penniless preacher from Nazareth is irrevocably the very center of history. Jesus Christ is the most dominant figure in all history." He also stated, "The doctrine of the Kingdom of Heaven, which was the main teaching of Jesus, is certainly one of the most revolutionary doctrines that ever stirred and changed human thought."[7]

Outside of all of this evidence, the New Testament writers were witnesses to their walk and faith in the Christ. They wrote about their experiences, which are now part of the Bible. The historical documentation is so strong that if you don't believe in the authenticity of Jesus based on past historical material, you have to question other prominent ancient figures such as Socrates, Plato, and Julius Caesar. Once one begins digging a little deeper, the evidence begins uncovering itself. Based on this evidence alone, the skeptics mentioned previously—Strobel, McDowell, and Wallace—continued their search. The history test was passed, so they moved on to the next question of interest.

Let's start with this—the evidence for the existence of Jesus is stronger than for any other ancient historical figure.

Chapter Six

WHO IS THIS
MAN JESUS?

W as Christ who He claimed to be? Was He God in human form? Why would God become human? Good questions. We have a loving, compassionate, and personal God who made Himself known to all by becoming human Himself.

Would there have been a better way to relate to humankind? I can't think of one. How could He know how we feel or truly understand us if He wasn't human Himself? To feel like a human, think like a human, be tempted like a human, and hurt like a human, you have to be a human. And so Christ, God of all ages, took on human form.

In *The Message*, Hebrews 2:14–18 explains:

Since the children are made of flesh and blood, it's logical that the Savior took on flesh and blood in order to rescue them by his death. By embracing death, taking it into himself, he destroyed the Devil's hold on death and freed all who cower through life, scared to death of death. It's obvious, of course, that he didn't go to all this trouble for angels. It was for people like us, children of Abraham. That's why he had to enter into every detail of human life. Then, when he came before God as high priest to get rid of the people's sins, he would have already experienced it all himself—all the pain, all the testing—and would be able to help where help was needed.

The Bridge between Man and God

Jesus was 100% man, so He could identify with us (feel our pain, temptations, and sorrows), and He was 100% God (representing the

Holiness of God) to take away the sins of our human failings. He was fully God *and* fully man (Colossians 1:19, 2:9). Philippians 2:6–8 gives a fuller explanation:

> *Have this attitude in yourselves which was also in Christ Jesus, who, as He already existed in the form of God, did not consider equality with God something to be grasped, but emptied Himself by taking the form of a bondservant and being born in the likeness of men. And being found in appearance as a man, He humbled Himself by becoming obedient to the point of death: death on a cross.*

Laying aside the privileges of deity, He personally sensed and experienced the humanness of each of us: pain, sorrow, weariness, and everything else human. But He was still God.

Our Christmas hymns speak of Immanuel. The word "Immanuel" means "God is with us." Isaiah 9:6 states, *"For a Child will be born to us, a Son will be given to us; and the government will rest on His shoulders; and His name will be called Wonderful Counselor, Mighty God, Eternal Father, Prince of Peace."* This baby born in Bethlehem was God Himself. He left Heaven to come to earth for both you and me. From the throne to the cross—could you think of any greater proof of God's personal love for you?

I have a little ornament as part of my Christmas decor that says, "He is the reason for the season." Christmas and Easter remind us of His birth, death, and resurrection. He is indeed the only One who is Holy and pure, the only one who can be the in-between bridge that connects the great divide between man, the hypocrite/sinner, and God.

He created you, and if He made you, you are valuable, despite the voices that tell you otherwise. Okay, heads up—here comes a biology lesson. This is a fun fact but an important one as well. You began as a seed—a sperm, to be exact. Did you know that you started in a competitive race? Three hundred million sperm are released, and during the race, 100 million of them tire out, but 200 million try to implant themselves into the human egg. This is so

important because … ta-daaaaaa … you won the race! Impressive sta-
tistics. You did it! You are priceless to Him!

**The thought in your head that tells you that you're any-
thing other than precious to Him is a lie.** It's a lie, it's a lie, it is a
lie! God loves you. Yes, you. The only voice that counts is the voice
of the One who created you, and when you read His Word, He tells
you that you are cherished by Him. So cherished that He paid for your
soul and made available eternal salvation in Heaven through the gift
of Himself. A gift to you, for you, and one that only you can accept
for yourself. You are priceless and so was His gift to you—salvation
through Jesus and Him alone. Salvation is free, but it wasn't cheap.
His death on the cross became a substitute: His righteousness for your
sinfulness. Acts 4:12 states, *"And there is salvation in no one else; for there
is no other name under heaven that has been given among mankind by which
we must be saved."*

Christ was both man and God. He was not some sort of demi-
god but fully God. He was tested and tempted as any man was, but He
came out without sin (2 Corinthians 5:21; Hebrews 4:15; 1 John 3:5).
First Peter 2:22 explains that Jesus was one, *"… who committed no sin,
nor was any deceit found in His mouth."*

However, Jesus didn't have access to all information. In His
humanness, He listened to the Father and did as He was instructed.
The Bible speaks of Christ coming to earth as an "advent," or an
arrival. The first advent occurred when He came to our world as a
baby. The second advent will take place when He comes as a triumphant King. In Matthew 24:36, the disciples ask Jesus about the timing
of His Second Coming to earth, or as stated in Isaiah 9:6, when the
"government will rest on His shoulders." He says that He doesn't know the
day or the hour. God the Father withheld this information from Jesus
in His humanity. There could be a multitude of reasons why God
reserved this knowledge from Jesus. Only He knows the reasons, and
they are for His purposes. If Jesus said that no one knows the hour or

the day, not even the angels in Heaven, then we know with absolute resolve that if anyone states a *specific* day, it will *not* happen on that day!

However, Jesus did explain the "generation" when He would arrive (which I'll explain in a later chapter). In Matthew 24, we're called to be prepared for Jesus' return at all times, because we do *not* know the day or hour of His return, or the day or hour of our own death. The world stage is completely set, and there is no time for preparation once He arrives. To be "ready" is to know (believe and receive) Jesus as your personal Saviour and Lord. He told us to watch for the signs, and they're here. Those with open eyes will see, and those who want to keep them closed will make that choice for themselves. These signs are undeniable if we know the Word of God, and they're standing right in front of us. God desires us to be prepared and ready. We don't need to fear if we know Jesus.

The only voice that counts is the voice of the One
who created you, and when you read His Word,
He tells you that you are cherished by Him.

The Messiah

The life story of the "Christ" was to be prophetically fulfilled. ("Christ" means Messiah. "Christ" was not his family name.) Back in the day, most Jewish people didn't recognize their Messiah, or "the Anointed One," because they were waiting for the One who would be a governing King to end all tyranny. Tyranny dripped daily on the streets of Jerusalem, and as long as the Romans were in charge, the Jewish people had no freedom. They were anxiously waiting for their saving and sword-bearing King who would end all their suffering.

Then Jesus shows up, and to their horror, they hear about the carpenter's son, dressed humbly, with no essence of majesty or dignity, and certainly with no wielding sword in hand, claiming to be the Messiah. The Jewish leaders just wanted Him gone. He was an embarrassment and a disgrace to the Jewish people. Rumblings began, causing unrest with both the Jews and Romans alike.

The New Testament describes what took place. The religious leaders asked Jesus outright if He was the Messiah, as explained in Mark 14:60–65: *"Again the high priest was questioning Him, and said to Him, 'Are You the Christ, the Son of the Blessed One?'"* (v. 61) They asked the question, but they only wanted a certain response. He answered them, *"I am; and you shall see the Son of Man sitting at the right hand of power, and coming with the clouds of heaven"* (v. 62). The priests were beside themselves; they tore their clothes and condemned Him as deserving of death. The very term "I am" was not only an answer to their question but a term God used to identify Himself. He is the great *"I AM"* (Exodus 3:7–8, 13–14*)*. When Jesus used this term, He did so deliberately. He is the "Son of Man" and the "Son of God." The Son of Man is referenced in Daniel 7:13–14, giving Him all authority, dominion, and the right to be worshipped.

At that time even His brothers didn't believe Him to be the Messiah, and they probably got a whiff of the priest's anger toward Jesus. They began thinking that He may be a little "off." Mark 3:21 lets us in on how they viewed Jesus: *"And when His own people heard about this, they came out to take custody of Him; for they were saying, 'He has lost His senses.'"* His "own" in this passage refers to His family. John 7:5 says, *"For not even His brothers believed in Him."* It wasn't until after the crucifixion, resurrection, and ascension that Jesus' brothers came to the knowledge of who He truly was. In Mark 3:31–32, we learn that Mary, Jesus' mother, was also with the brothers that day. I will surmise that Mary was either instructed by God not to try and convince Jesus' half-brothers and sisters of whom she knew Him to be, or perhaps she'd made a decision that each of her children would need to make their own choice. Then she lifted up her children in prayer.

The Old Testament describes the Messiah as a future Kingdom-leader to end all tyranny but also as a suffering Servant. The Jewish people wanted their leader (Messiah) to revolt against the

Romans immediately. Many were blinded to the fact that He also came to suffer and die for the sins of humanity, even though this was clearly taught in the Old Testament. However, the Jews who chose to follow Jesus Christ as their Lord, basing their faith on the entirety of Old Testament prophecies about their Messiah, recognized Jesus, accepted Him as their Saviour, and became known as Christians (Christ-followers). Christianity began with the Jewish believers first (Romans 1:16).

Then many disciples and followers of Jesus took the good news of the "gospel" (simple acronym: **G**-God's **O**-only **S**-Son, **P**-perished to give us **E**–everlasting, **L**-Life [John 3:16]) to the Gentile world, so the free gift of God (Romans 6:23) would be a gift for the entire world and not just for the Jews. Their Jewish Messiah would be the suffering Servant (this would be Christ's first coming to earth), dying on the cross for the sins of humanity. In time, He would be a world Kingdom-leader (second coming of Christ to earth).

The New Testament wasn't written until years after the resurrection, so all the scripture that pointed to the Messiah as a suffering Servant and triumphant King came strictly from the Hebrew Bible (or the Old Testament). This is the same Old Testament that both the present-day Jews and we as Christians read today. But back in the day, those searching for their Messiah wouldn't have had access to instant answers, and they didn't have the Internet to look things up. If they wanted to look up scripture about their Messiah, if they believed Jesus to be Him, the priests would have to remember hundreds of pieces of scripture and where they were found. However, even when Jesus and the disciples did point out the Old Testament promises and prophecies, many people hardened their hearts. In John 5:39, Jesus challenged them: *"You examine the Scriptures because you think that in them you have eternal life; and it is those very Scriptures that testify about Me."* Their Scripture pointed directly to Jesus, yet they couldn't see, or they chose not to see. Hmm ... to see or not to see, that is the question! I'm not sure if things have changed that much.

*It wasn't until after the crucifixion, resurrection,
and ascension that Jesus' brothers came to the
knowledge of who He truly was.*

Fulfillment of Prophecy

So why don't the Jews of today look to Jesus as their Messiah? Actually, some do. Messianic Jews have studied the Old Testament scriptures to identify the prophecies, and they have embraced Jesus as the fulfillment of those prophecies and accepted Him as their Messiah and Lord. The author of *The Harbinger*, Jonathan Cahn; author/speaker Amir Tsarfati; and Jonathan Bernis, President and CEO of Jewish Voice Ministries are some of today's well-known Jewish believers of Jesus.

In the *Day of Discovery's* DVD *My Search for the Messiah*, Dr. Michael Rydelnik shares his story. He was on a mission to disprove his mother's beliefs that Jesus was their Jewish Messiah. His mother was a Holocaust survivor, and he was outraged and determined to point out the error of her ways. He began a concentrated study of his Hebrew Bible, the Tanach. But as he extensively researched, he found that the Jewish Messiah pointed to the fulfilled prophecies of Jesus. When introduced to his Old Testament scripture pointing out dozens of accurate prophesies fulfilled, he came to the realization that Jesus was who He claimed to be—the Messiah.

Jesus (or "Yeshua" in Hebrew) is the Jewish Messiah and is not hidden in the Old Testament. Yet today most Jews don't see that this man of humility could also be their future sword-bearing King. Just as we don't always recognize others for their true worth, they too could not recognize that a King may have hidden beneath a servant's clothes. Nor could they (or we) see that an Oxford don sometimes wardrobes himself in gardener's attire.

However, those who study the Old Testament prophecies clearly see the dual role of their Jewish Servant/King, as well as our Gentile Saviour. He was and is both the suffering Servant, the Passover

"Lamb" that takes away the sins of the world, and the "Lion" from the tribe of Judah. That Lion will one day make His appearance to the whole world at His Second Coming: *"Behold, He is coming with the clouds, and every eye will see Him, even those who pierced Him; and all the tribes of the earth will mourn over Him. So it is to be. Amen"* (Revelation 1:7). The suffering Servant comes *before* the reigning King. There are not two Messiahs, but one. The fulfillment of Jewish prophecy is one of the most remarkable pieces of evidence that proves that the Bible is the Word of God.

We will look at the exponential impossibilities of all this happening by chance in a further chapter that will blow you away! If all prophecies were fulfilled at the first showtime of the Jewish Messiah, we need to be cognizant that His second appearance will also occur.

I have heard that the New Testament reveals what the Old Testament concealed. It confirms the prophecies of the Old, fulfilled through the life of Jesus Christ. Often the Old Testament readers couldn't decipher what the scriptures meant because the prophecies hadn't come to pass. It was a mystery until the New Testament fulfillment of the prophecies came along. Then the puzzle pieces shifted naturally, and more importantly, without human manipulation.

Old Testament prophets craved to know more about their Jewish Messiah, but they weren't privy to that information. We are given insight to their desire:

> *As to this salvation, the prophets who prophesied of the grace that would come to you made careful searches and inquiries, seeking to know what person or time the Spirit of Christ within them was indicating as He predicted the sufferings of Christ and the glories to follow. It was revealed to them that they were not serving themselves, but you, in these things which have now been announced to you through those who preached the gospel to you by the Holy Spirit sent from heaven—things into which angels long to look.*
>
> —1 Peter 1:10–12

Often the scribes of the Old Testament were writing about future events that weren't even on their radar screen. The crucifixion would be one example of a prophecy written hundreds of years before it originated. Can you imagine how the writers of these prophecies must have processed some of this information? Sometimes I picture the Old Testament scribes with quills in hand, aggressively rubbing their bald heads, looking up into the heavens and asking, "Yahweh, are You *sure* I got this right?"

Part Two

THE MIDDLE GROUND

Chapter Seven

JESUS AND WORLDVIEWS

Let's begin to look at Christ's claim that He was the only way to Father God. John 14:6 states, *"Jesus said to Him, 'I am the way, and the truth, and the life; no one comes to the Father except through Me.'"* Saying you are the only way to God the Father is not a popular viewpoint by any stretch, and I can't win any popularity contest echoing that statement. That is a strong and defiant declaration that Jesus made to the world, yet He made it. He was the ultimate rebel with a cause. He proclaimed that there is only one way to God, and it is through Him. Such a bold statement, but one each of us will choose to accept or reject.

We all want to be right in our ideas and formulated concepts— ones that make us feel comfortable with our life and, frankly, our lifestyle. But Jesus never made anyone feel comfortable, and that's the truth of it. He was radical and shook the then-known world. People hated Him because He called them out. Jesus challenged them, and He probed their hearts, minds, and actions. He is no different today, which is why a good portion of us would rather ignore Him. It is never easy to change. Change and transition can be difficult, but they can also be life-giving!

The Way, the Truth, and the Life

Can all roads lead to Heaven? Some very prominent religious leaders today say they can. They believe that all religions and beliefs, at their core, take different avenues but convene in Heaven.

However, it's crucial to note that these leaders also don't believe in biblical inerrancy. It's an obvious conclusion, then, that those who don't believe in the Word of God as being inerrant—the Holy and true Word of God, incapable of being wrong—teach the opposite of what God has recorded and written for the world to see: that there is one way to Heaven.

The statement *"I am the way, and the truth, and the life; no one comes to the Father but through Me"* offers us hope. If we believe that God's Word is true, we will use that as our plumbline for our worldview. If we don't believe in God's Word, we embrace whatever suits us best.

There were ancient cults and religions that sacrificed human beings to their demon gods. Should demon worship qualify anyone to get into Heaven? Human sacrifice … yikes! I don't know about you, but I'm glad I didn't attend that church! Jesus teaches us to respect life, and human sacrifice doesn't fall under that category.

Think about this: how can both points of view be correct? Human sacrifice (practised by the Ancient Mayans and other ancient cults, as well as some worship practices today) and respecting life (practised by the Judeo-Christian faith) are polar-opposite viewpoints.

So do all roads lead to Heaven? How can two opposing views be correct? Sacrificing a child, or any human, opposes the idea that all human lives are of value in God's creation. This should cause us to sit down and question our acceptance of embracing every viewpoint that chimes, "All roads lead to Heaven."

The Bible teaches us what is right and wrong, and they are called absolutes. What qualifies anyone for Heaven is a purifying link that cleanses all sin. When we know Christ and His saving grace, He can indeed, make the vilest sinner clean. It is the cross, not us, that makes us flawless.

C.S. Lewis once said that Jesus was either a liar, a lunatic, or Lord. Forget the good guy or being a great teacher stuff; Jesus didn't give us that option. His life, love, and actions were the opposite of what a liar or lunatic would produce. He changed the course of morality in human history, and you cannot hand that baton over to someone who consistently lies or is a crazy person. If you fully explore those possibilities, everything He said and fulfilled supported the fact that He was Lord. In his book *Mere Christianity*, C.S. Lewis expands on this reasoning:

> I am trying here to prevent the really foolish thing that people often say about Him: I'm ready to accept Jesus as a great moral teacher, but I don't accept his claim to be God. That is the one thing we must not say. A man who was merely a man and said the sort of things Jesus said would not be a great moral teacher. He would either be a lunatic—on the level with the man who says he is a poached egg—or else he would be the Devil of Hell. You must make your choice. Either this man was, and is, the Son of God, or else a madman or something worse. You can shut him up for a fool, you can spit at him and kill him as a demon or you can fall at his feet and call him Lord and God, but let us not come with any patronizing nonsense about his being a great human teacher. He has not left that open to us. He did not intend to.[8]

Individually, we need to make a personal choice about who Jesus is. To ignore making a choice is making a choice.

An authentic choice needs evaluation. It's a decision we need to make. A person cannot believe in multiple gods and one God simultaneously. These are opposites: one is right, and the other is wrong. Universalism teaches that whatever we want to believe in is truth for us and that all roads will take us to God, a god, or our personal belief system—just because we believe it to be so. But eternity, according to God's Word, does not revolve around our personal bents or subjective sincerity. If God is God, then we are not.

I've heard it said that the Christian faith is one of exclusivity. Other religions, not just Christianity, claim exclusivity. However, I believe that Christianity is the most inclusive religion anyone could ever come across (I will use the term "religion" here, but for myself and other believers in Christ, it is a relationship). Coming to a personal faith in Jesus includes anyone, anytime, anywhere! You don't have to earn, bargain, or work for it. It's free. The saving grace of Jesus Christ is immediate upon one's genuine salvation prayer to accept Him into their lives and heart. Christianity is the only religion that teaches that Heaven isn't earned by merit or favour (Ephesians 2:8–9). That is in stark contrast to all world religions.

Worldviews Shape and Define Us

Our individual worldview shapes and defines us. It's the lens we look through as we view our world, and it becomes our measuring stick for our ethics, morality, and beliefs. From this, we begin to treat others, our world, and ourselves accordingly.

There are at least four defining categories to assess worldviews: origin, meaning, morality, and destiny.

Origin—Where do we come from? How did we originate?

Meaning—What is our value and worth? Why do we have worth? Who gives us worth? Does our life have meaning?

Morality—Where does our intrinsic moral code come from? Who has the authority to create and shape our moral ethics?

Destiny—What does our destiny and future hold? Who is in control? What does eternity encompass for each of us?

As we look through the lens of our belief system, we must ask ourselves these questions. Only Jesus, through His payment for us on the cross, can envelope all the answers to the above questions. In Jesus, our *origin* stems from a Mighty Creator. Our *meaning*, value, and worth are inherited by us from Him. Our *morality* is shaped by a moral compass called the Bible, and our *destiny* of eternal life is secured because of Jesus' death on the cross—not because of good works or our own doing. And it is solely and "soul-ly" because of Him.

When we know Jesus, our eternity is Heaven-bound, and our desires will be God-honouring. In the book *Heaven*, Randy Alcorn writes:

We'll have many desires in Heaven, but they won't be unholy desires. Everything we want will be good. Our desires will please God. All will be right with the world, nothing forbidden ... Christianity is unique in its perspective of our desires, teaching that they will be sanctified and fulfilled on the New Earth. Conversely, the Buddhist concept of deliverance teaches that one day people's desires will be eliminated. That's radically different. Christianity teaches that Jesus takes our sins away while redeeming our desires.[9]

Our individual self will continue in Heaven, only without the baggage of sin weighing us down, and that promise can surely bring hope to the hopeless. That hope comes through Christ Jesus' substitutionary payment for our sin on the cross. Bruce Milne explains that death doesn't have to destroy those who know Jesus:

We can banish all fear of being absorbed into the "All" which Buddhism holds before us, or reincarnated in some other life form as in the post-modern prospect of Hinduism ... The self with which we were endowed by the Creator in his gift of life to us, the self whose worth was secured forever in the self-substitution of God for us on the cross, that self will endure into eternity. Death cannot destroy us.[10]

Hope is anchored and secured through Jesus Christ. Our hope goes beyond ourselves because we personally know a benevolent God. We will receive new bodies and renewed minds in Heaven. What joy that can bring to those who suffer physically here on earth. Joni Eareckson Tada was seventeen years old when she became a quadriplegic due to a diving accident. She speaks for many when she looks forward to a new body in Heaven:

I still can hardly believe it. I, with shriveled, bent fingers, atrophied muscles, gnarled knees, and no feeling from the shoulders down, will one day have a new body, light, bright, and clothed in righteousness—powerful and dazzling. Can you imagine the hope this gives someone spinal-cord injured like me? Or someone who is cerebral palsied, brain-injured, or who has multiple sclerosis? Imagine the hope this gives someone who is manic-depressive. No other world religion, no other philosophy promises new bodies, hearts, and minds. Only in the Gospel of Christ do hurting people find such incredible hope.[11]

That Heaven, through Christ's salvation alone, is offered to each of us, and no other world religion can offer that eternal security.

Image-Bearers

Being image-bearers of God shapes our meaning, value, and worth. God created humankind, and He created animal-kind. There was no biological hiccup in which He mixed up each set of genetics. According to the Word of God, it's not a choice we make: God already made it for us as humans. We are His image-bearers (Genesis 1:26–27). However, the world will say differently because they don't use the Bible as a reference point. If we trust God's Word as truly being His Word, we have a moral compass. I don't have to figure it out based on my feelings or thoughts. Guidelines are made and given through Him.

But the world is telling us otherwise. I heard an interview with a person who identified himself with wolves and wanted to hang out with them (he didn't explain how he did that without getting torn to shreds) because of his "inner wolf." I mean no disrespect to this person, because this is their belief, but we need to be aware that this is what the world is feeding individuals and our children. Public schools are telling children that they can be anything they want to be, including animals, and not in a cutesy way. They allow them to dress up as the animal they "identify" with. I recently heard a story of a young boy who identified as a dog and had a leash and wanted to be led around in school with it. I don't want to know what he did about the bathroom situation!

This is a form of Darwinism—the belief that we are a part of the animal species. With Darwinism in and biblical principles out, and without faith in the God of the Bible, this type of news may be alarming to us, but it won't be surprising. Without a moral compass, we get off course. Without God's guidelines, we make up our own. The deterioration begins when we become biblically malnourished and no longer see God as our Creator, and us as His creation. God calls humankind His image-bearers.

Perhaps you think that the Bible's boundaries and precepts are irrelevant today. God tells us differently. People and society may change, but God never changes (Numbers 23:19; Hebrews 13:8; Malachi 3:6; James 1:17). His boundaries and laws are there for a reason; even though you may disagree with them or Him, He is God, and He knows better. As Creator of the universe and the intricate Designer of your soul and body, He knows what's best for His creation. I've seen how far off-track humans are going, and as we keep pushing God out of the picture, it will get a lot worse. Without a biblical moral imprint in our hearts, all things become subjective morality and a matter of opinion. If you haven't heard this already, opinions are like belly buttons—everyone has one!

Three-in-One

We are introduced to the Triune God right at the starting gate. In the first chapter of the Bible, we find out why we have value and worth. We are the image-bearers of God! Genesis 1:26 says, "*Then God said, 'Let Us make mankind in Our image, according to Our likeness ...'*" Notice the plural pronouns. "Us" and "Our" point to the Triune God—the three-in-one God: Father, Son, and Holy Spirit.

The word "Trinity" is not in the Bible, but strong references point to one, and a triune Being is mentioned throughout its entirety. The Old and New Testaments reference the Son and the Holy Spirit as being part of the Trinity many times over. Right off the hop,

Genesis 1:2b states, *"the Spirit of God was hovering over the surface of the waters."* As talked about in an earlier chapter, the word "Immanuel" (Isaiah 7:14) means "God is with us" and speaks of the Child that will be born to us and the Son that will be given (Isaiah 9:6), calling Him "Mighty God" and "Eternal Father." That Child and Son are given titles that reference God Himself. A multitude of verses point to the three-in-one God. Thomas exclaims, "My Lord and my God!" when he sees Jesus after the resurrection, and Jesus doesn't stop him from his acknowledgment or worship. Jesus forgave people of their sins, and as only God can forgive sins, this indicated that Jesus was God. The religious leaders took that and ran, believing it to be the ammunition they needed to begin plans for His death. Before Jesus ascended to Heaven, He addressed His disciples (and us) in Matthew 28:16–20, saying, *"Go, therefore, and make disciples of all the nations, baptizing them in the name of the Father and the Son and the Holy Spirit …"* (v. 19).

Personally, I've never struggled with God being a triune Being. I've always related the three-in-one relationship to the way we, as humans, are designed to be. This doesn't come from a deep theological study about this subject but from how I personally view the triune relationship. I often hear others make the best possible comparisons of triune (tri-unity) examples to something physical on earth—a three-leaf clover; an egg with a shell, white, and yolk; or water that moves into different stages of ice, steam, and liquid.

Outside of Christianity, all other faiths teach that God cannot be a three-in-one Being, so they can't accept Jesus as being God. But if we are His image-bearers, and He said He would make man (humankind) in "Our" image, we can push further into what a tri-unity being may look like.

I believe that God the Father, Son, and Holy Spirit are Soul (which consists of mind, will, and emotions), Body, and Spirit. Each of us is soul, body, and spirit too. In the soul, we have a mind, will, and emotions; we also have a body and a spirit. We too are tri-unity beings, but we are *not* God and never will be gods. That is critical to note, as a number of religions today teach that becoming a god is our eventual and final state. Only God is God and will remain to be so for all eternity.

Often my mind reasons with my body, especially when I don't want to do something but know I should, or the other way around. At times my spirit can war with my fleshly desires, and sometimes I have all three going at once. I argue with my triune self because of sinfulness; however, God, Jesus, and Holy Spirit are sinless and work in unity. In His humanness, Jesus wrestled with dying on the cross and cried out to God the Father in the Garden of Gethsemane, but He completed His prayer by saying, "Thy will be done." Father, Son, and Holy Spirit worked together in harmony to achieve salvation for the human race. They worked on our behalf.

There is a warring and a wrestling that goes on within each of us, and sometimes I become defeated. It becomes an internal struggle. I have prayed over a matter and not moved forward on things I should have. There are periods when I haven't slowed down long enough to hear His voice. At other times, I didn't care for others' needs because of my busyness. My internal sparring goes on, and sometimes I become confused about what the right option may be. But at other times it becomes clear, and "Thy will be done" becomes my answer too. It is here, where the three-in-one unite, that I begin to do God's will in my life. And it is here where I have borne more Christ to others than self.

As humans, we flounder and fail, and sometimes we just don't know how things will pan out in our lives. I have found that there are periods in our lives when we can't see ahead and just need to keep going. One day I heard a great sermon that helped me begin to navigate and gravitate toward the right steps. It was an easy pace, and when I was too tired and couldn't see my future plans or which path to take, it encouraged me to keep one foot in front of the other. To continue on the righteous road, and when you don't know what else to do, simply: 1) do what is right (according to the Word); and 2) trust

God. If that is all we do, we're walking in the correct direction toward the lane of obedience.

As a complete unit of soul, body, and spirit, we are creations of God. God can shape and mold our lives accordingly if we trust that we are His image-bearers. It is here, as image-bearers, where our morality is not a matter of guesswork but is given to us in the Word of God. There is good, and there is evil; there is right, and there is wrong. Here in Christ, the Incarnate Word (1 John 1), we find security, we find our bearings, and we find our paths.

Uncertainty No More

World religions are uncertain in their teachings about how to enter Heaven, Nirvana, or whatever they may call their afterlife. They have to pay the price in some way on their own merit, so they reach up and do, do, do. But with Jesus Christ's payment on the cross, God reaches down and says, "*Done!*" Paid. Wiped Out. Forgiven. When Jesus died on the cross, His last words were, "It is finished." His physical death was finished, but His spiritual work—salvation through any other means but Him—was finished as well.

Let's explore a bit further. Many major world religions are based on a vision or visions given to one person, with no witnesses around to testify to that vision. In that case, we trust one person's viewpoint and the writings about their encounter. Here are only a handful of views:

Buddhism—a vision given to one man, Buddha (Siddhartha Guatama), with no other witnesses, follows a search for inner spiritual enlightenment, a personal quest for peace with no pursuit toward God. There is no belief in God but instead a "oneness" with everything. *Either there is a God or there is no God. These are opposite teachings.*

Islam—a vision given to one man named Muhammed (or Mohammed), who, according to the Muslim faith, was the greatest prophet of all prophets. The Muslims worship one being—Allah. They state that Jesus is only a prophet and can't be God or Saviour of the world. *Either Jesus is just a prophet or He is God as He claimed to be. These are opposite claims.*

Hindus—have millions of gods and goddesses (some have proposed up to 333 million) that all serve a different purpose. Within the law of karma, there is no possibility of wiping the slate clean but instead there are consequences for our actions. *Either we suffer for the consequences of our mistakes or we are given freedom from sin through Christ's atonement. These are opposite outcomes.*

Mormonism—believe that Joseph Smith was visited by an angel who gave him information to begin to write the Book of Mormon. He peered into a hat with seer stones in it so that he could translate the words into English. *Either the Book of Mormon or the Holy Bible is God's Word. These are opposite belief systems.*

These religions are far from an exhaustive list and have opposing beliefs that cannot equally be true. We need to choose. One of the main differences between the Christian Scriptures and those of other faiths is that the Bible is not based on *one* person's ideals or visions. The Bible is a comprehensive gathering of multiple writers, throughout many centuries, with literally hundreds of prophecies fulfilled (and some yet to come), yet it makes one cohesive story—humanity's fall and then redemption made possible by none other than God Himself.

There was a price tag placed on Christ for you to get into Heaven, and you don't have to buy it, earn it, or pay for it. It has been taken care of, bought, and paid for at a hefty price. Accepting Jesus as one's Lord and Saviour is all that needs to be done. One can pray, meditate, and do good works through world religions, but none of this unlocks the entrance to Heaven itself. Only through Jesus are our sins covered. Because of Him, we can enter the gates of Heaven and into the fullness of a Holy, pure, and righteous God. Our hope for eternal life is secured through Him.

In Psalm 4:2, God speaks: "*How long will you people turn my glory into shame? How long will you love delusions and seek false gods?*" (NIV). Can all religions be right, even though they contradict each other? I get that these tough questions challenge us, but it's better to face them and answer them here instead of face to face with Him one day. If our God is Holy, just, and righteous, all roads cannot lead to Heaven. Through religion we bring our sinfulness before a pure God, trying to earn His favour. However, if our sins are atoned for through the blood of God Himself (Could there be any other substitute more qualified and pure?), then we too can stand in righteousness before Him. God gives boundaries and standards, and just as there are earthly laws and boundaries, so there are spiritual laws and boundaries.

Only through Jesus are our sins covered. Because of Him, we can enter the gates of Heaven and into the fullness of a Holy, pure, and righteous God. Our hope for eternal life is secured through Him.

Chapter Eight

THE UNIQUENESS
OF THE BIBLE

I recently heard a woman voicing (no, I should say screaming) her opinion on the Internet, stating that the Bible is a mythical book, yet she had no evidence. How can one make such a statement without reading or studying it? I'm amazed at how many people hold that viewpoint without a generous study of God's Word. Either they've adopted it from others or they just assume it to be true without researching and weighing the evidence. We may not want to believe things written in the Bible, or we may even want to go our own way once we know it, but the Bible has stood on its own and has proven to be the Word of God in more ways than we could imagine! Historically, geologically, and archeologically, it's a match. The numbers of writers that make up a cohesive story, as well as hundreds of fulfilled prophecies, eyewitness accounts, and testimonies of seeing Jesus after the resurrection—a match to the Old and New Testament! Creation alone speaks of a Creator, and then there are the transformed lives. These are only some of the ways God has made Himself known to us.

The Word is inerrant. God wants to be found and known by you. He has supplied more than ample evidence. If the "ears" of our hearts are closed, we could bring unending evidence to the table, but it will not be "heard." It won't do a thing if we're closed to hearing Him speak to us. If this is you, perhaps asking God to make your heart pliable enough to listen would be a good start, and just see what He can do with that.

The Bible is outstanding, unique, and distinctly different from any other religious book. "Scripture" means inspired writings, and it's God-breathed. In 2 Timothy 3:16, Paul explains: "*All Scripture is inspired by God and profitable for teaching, for rebuke, for correction, for training in righteousness.*" Jesus verifies the trustworthiness of the Old Testament by often stating, "Scripture says ..." and quoting from three-quarters of those books. In doing so, He testifies that they are the words of a Holy God. Those inspired words flowed through the pens of multiple writers, who recorded what was spoken to them by God Himself.

Scribes, Books, Years, and Continents

One of the first things that makes the Bible's writings authentic compared to other religious holy books is diversity. It took approximately forty scribes to write the Bible, but it has one Author, making up sixty-six books over a 1,500-year period, and it was written on three continents. The Old and New Testaments blend to make one connected story—redemption for humankind through Christ alone.

How could it possibly be that random people throughout multiple centuries came up with bits and pieces of writings to make a cohesive book? How can it be that prophetic words were written in different centuries and throughout different continents yet can give the world great precision and accuracy in their foretelling? How can it be that hundreds of prophetic utterings could come to pass exactly as proclaimed, as well as provide the timing of the Jewish Messiah's first arrival on earth? The answer is because it is truth, God's truth, given to us in His Word.

Prophecy is one of the most extraordinary pieces of evidence that the Bible is God's truth. No other religious book can give you this type of accuracy and faultless precision in prophecies, with some being documented one thousand or more years before they happened. The men who transcribed what the Lord told them to write would never see the things they penned come to pass, or even be aware that those things could exist in the future.

We've seen that many world religions are based on one person's visions and writings. In a court of law, having other witnesses testify to the truth is helpful. One person's viewpoint may be trustworthy, but how can we know for sure unless others are there as well? The fact that the Bible had multiple writers, and those stories became fashioned together to make a comprehensive, accurate, and deliberate foretelling of Jesus, is simply remarkable!

How could it possibly be that random people throughout multiple centuries came up with bits and pieces of writings to make a cohesive book?

The Resurrection

The second and most significant confirmation of the Christian faith is the resurrected body of Jesus Christ. The leaders of world religions have burial sites, but they never claimed that they would rise from the dead. Jesus' body was never found because He arose on the third day, just as He said He would (Mark 9:30–32; Matthew 17:22–23). Archeologists have yet to discover the body of Jesus!

In Josh McDowell's book *The New Evidence That Demands a Verdict*, he explains, "The resurrection of Jesus Christ and Christianity stand or fall together."[12] Many people throughout history have emphatically said that the resurrection was a hoax. Josh McDowell debates this statement and gives evidence to the contrary. It's a good reminder to insert here that Josh McDowell was not a Christian but a skeptic when he began researching this type of material. He builds a solid and sturdy case for readers. I recommend this read for complex and curious inquiries about the Christian faith. It's filled with difficult questions and great and powerful answers. The thought of the resurrection being a hoax is discussed in great detail, and he gives excellent answers to those who question it.

From Jesus' day to the present, religious leaders and others have taught that there is no such thing as the resurrection of the dead. This confused believers. The Sadducees were a Jewish sect that didn't believe in the resurrection of the dead—so that's why they were sad, you see? (Sorry, I couldn't resist.) On a more serious note, many people today believe that once we die, that's it. We're done and gone. That is not what Jesus taught. His resurrection taught us that there is life after death.

The heartiest piece of evidence of the uniqueness of Christianity is the resurrection. All of the Christian faith hinges on this. You can't have an authentic Christian faith without believing that Jesus Christ rose from the dead. The apostle Paul explains why it is so crucial in 1 Corinthians 15:12–14:

> *Now if Christ is preached, that He has been raised from the dead, how do some among you say that there is no resurrection of the dead? But if there is no resurrection of the dead, then not even Christ has been raised, and if Christ has not been raised, then our preaching is in vain, your faith also is in vain.*

If one doesn't believe in the inerrancy of the Bible, one will come up with different thoughts about Jesus and His resurrection. However, there is sufficient evidence that stands on its own and points to a resurrected Jesus. People have argued that Christ "swooned" (became unconscious) on the cross and was placed in the tomb. Later, the disciples stole His body. If one knows the history of the Roman soldiers and the price they would pay for a bad day at work, one would know that there was no wiggle room to be slack on any post. Roman soldiers were trained to ensure that the bodies of any crucifixion deaths were dead before the body was removed. They were experts in capital punishment.

Jesus had up to thirty-nine lashes, but some say it could have been more than that because the Romans were not necessarily following the Jewish law of "forty minus one" (Deuteronomy 25:3). The whip was made to tear the flesh open. It wasn't just a leather whip, but one with shards attached to cut and tear purposefully. The tearing of the flesh and the blood loss alone could cause death. Isaiah 53 was written some seven hundred years before Jesus came to earth and is packed full of prophecies about His beatings, bruising, and crucifixion.

We know He carried His cross for some period of time, according to the book of John (John 19:16–18), and then He was nailed to the cross. The Roman soldiers couldn't leave a site until the crucified were dead. If they needed to get someone off the cross after a certain amount of time, they would break their legs to quicken their death. The victims wouldn't be able to hold themselves up on the cross and would die of suffocation quickly.

These soldiers were very familiar with what death looked like following a crucifixion. In the case of Jesus, the soldier could see that He was already dead and didn't break his legs. John, one of Jesus' disciples, was at the crucifixion. As he testifies in John 19:36: "*For these things took place so that the Scripture would be fulfilled: 'Not a bone of Him shall be broken.'*" This was an Old Testament Messianic prophecy stated in Psalm 34:20 and Numbers 9:12. The Jewish Passover lamb (Exodus 12) was replaced by the true Passover Lamb, Jesus Christ. In John 1:29b, John the Baptist tells the world, "*Behold, the Lamb of God, who takes away the sins of the world!*" The unbroken bones of Jesus become the fruition and completion of the pure, Holy, and sacrificial Passover Lamb.

Without breaking His legs, the Roman soldiers ensured that Jesus was dead by driving a spear through His side to puncture both the lungs and His heart. If He was alive and His heart was beating, it would have pulsated blood with every beat until he died. The Old Testament foretelling claimed this piercing would happen to the suffering Servant in Zechariah 12:10. It's recorded in John 19:31–37 that blood and water came out of Jesus' side when He was pierced, so on all levels, we know He was completely and utterly dead. The flow of blood and water fulfills another scripture in Psalm 22:14 where it tells us His heart became like wax, and it did just that—it poured out like wax.

Other bystanders watched, so by all accounts, there were several eyewitnesses to testify of His death. A wealthy man named Joseph of Arimathea requested that Jesus' body be taken off the cross and buried in his own personal tomb hewn into a rock cave. Pilate wanted to reassure himself that Jesus was dead and questioned the centurion personally (Mark 15:42–46). Only then did Pilate release the body over to Joseph,

Instead of Jesus' body being thrown into the pile of the crucified, Joseph of Arimathea relinquished his tomb to Jesus, fulfilling yet another Old Testament prophecy. Isaiah 53 tells the story of Jesus' suffering in detail, and Isaiah 53:9 explains, *"And His grave was assigned with wicked men, yet He was with a rich man in His death ..."* When Jesus was taken off the cross, Joseph and Nicodemus took Him to the site of the burial tomb. They wrapped the body of Jesus tightly, as well as over the face, nose, and body, along with about seventy-five pounds of spice (John 19:38–41). For those who may have the slightest doubt that this all wasn't enough to make sure He was dead, the weight of the spices and the tight wrapping would have ensured it was impossible to escape from an earthly and physical body—but not from a resurrected one!

Before Jesus was buried, the chief priest and the Pharisees were fearful because it was rumoured that He'd claimed that He would rise from the dead in three days (Mark 9:30–32; Matthew 17:22–23). The religious leaders didn't want Him gaining any more followers than He already had. They wanted the rumour to die along with Jesus and to ensure that no disciples would be stealing His body. They believed that if the disciples succeeded and circulated that Jesus was alive, it would cause quite the buzz. However, in the disciples' grief, they forgot that Christ spoke of His resurrection (John 20:9). The Jewish leaders, however, did not.

The leaders went to Pilate and insisted that Jesus' tomb be guarded (Matthew 27:62–66), and Pilate gave the orders for the tomb to be safeguarded. Pilate responds to them by saying, "You have your guard go, make it as secure as you know how." A Roman "guard" would consist of two men, and others would be needed for sleep shifts. In order to seal the tomb, many soldiers were required. Some historians mention between thirty to fifty Roman guards to move the stone and ensure security.

In Matthew 27:57–60, we read about Joseph and the stone placement over the tomb. In verse 60, it mentions that Joseph rolled the stone in front of the tomb; we can know that Joseph did not do this by himself. There are examples in history that support this, such as King Solomon "building" the first temple. We know King Solomon may have overseen the project, but he himself would not do the work. Joseph was a man of wealth and had others do his work. By this we know that Joseph would not have rolled the stone into place by himself. He would have either instructed the soldiers when the body was completely wrapped and placed, or perhaps in humble respect, he helped to roll the stone into place along with the soldiers. The soldiers rolled a massive stone to block the entrance, saying to have weighed about four thousand pounds, then placed a Roman wax seal over the stone to deter anyone from breaking in. A person breaking the wax seal was guaranteed severe Roman punishment.[13]

Guarding a tomb against robbery was more than just a job. If any soldier was slack while guarding a prisoner, and the prisoner escaped, it would cost them their life. No matter how tired they would have been at the end of their work shift, losing their life for a bad day's work was not a regular occurrence. The Roman guards held this job with the utmost respect. Only the resurrection could have let them fail in their task! The security measures were tight. Because the religious leaders wanted to make sure this body wasn't stolen, there is strong belief that the Jewish Temple guards would have joined the watch as well. At any rate, there was enough dedicated staff to ensure that neither the disciples nor others could have rolled away the stone and taken the body.

Reading Matthew 28 tells us the rest of the story, what they saw, and what happened afterward. A great earthquake shakes the place, an angel descends and rolls away the stone, and they "became like dead men." When they recover, they rush into the city and tell the Jewish leaders all that happened, and their lives are spared. The fact that they lived is testimony in and of itself to the resurrection. They should have been killed for sloppy workmanship; instead, they found protection under the wings of the Jewish priests. There must have been an enormous amount of shock and terror on both their faces and bodies for the priests to read their body language, believe they were telling the truth, and spare their lives. The Jewish higher-ups obviously trusted it to be a genuine confession; otherwise, they wouldn't have protected them *and* paid them off to lie. To the guards, it was sheer terror, but to others, the rolled-away stone meant the dawn of a new morning that radiated hope for the entire world! The resurrected body of Jesus proved His claims that He is God Incarnate (John 8:58, 10:30).

The Resurrected Christ on Earth

You can imagine the hopelessness and despair over the crucifixion for those who knew Jesus, and the restored hope and courage that the resurrection brought. In John 20, Jesus meets with the disciples after the resurrection has taken place. But it wasn't only the disciples He appeared to; over five hundred eyewitnesses saw Him after the resurrection and observed the nail-scarred appendages. He didn't just appear to the disciples and His family; others also gave testimony of seeing Jesus alive, and that transformed their lives. And *all* of them had the same experience of seeing a nail-pierced resurrected Christ walking the earth, which would disqualify them from having a "hallucination," as referred to in an earlier chapter. Hallucinations would never be precisely the same for over five hundred individuals.

Paul explains in 1 Corinthians 15:6–8:

After that He appeared to more than five hundred brothers and sisters at one time, most of whom remain until now, but some have fallen asleep; then He appeared to James, then to all the apostles and last of all, as to one untimely born, He appeared to me also.

Before he encountered Jesus, Paul instigated the killing of Christians and, in doing so, hoped to kill their faith—that is, until Christ got a hold of him. His conversion was so dramatic and dynamic that Paul (previously named Saul until his conversion) wrote more books of the New Testament than any other apostle.

Jesus was on the earth for forty days following the resurrection. Acts 1:3 tells us, *"To these He also presented Himself alive after His suffering, by many convincing proofs, appearing to them over a period of forty days and speaking of things regarding the kingdom of God."* Jesus' appearance changed the lives of the believers and proved beyond doubt that He had been raised from the dead. You can't be a coward one day and preach the gospel the next *unless* a transformation has taken place.

In John 20:19–30, we read about Jesus being among the disciples. These observers saw Him; some ate with Him, and even doubting Thomas was told to touch Him and examine His scars and wounds. Thomas responded with, "My Lord and my God." Christ allowed Himself to be worshipped by Thomas; He did not stop it. Jesus addresses Thomas and us when He speaks in John 20:29: *"Because you have seen Me, have you now believed? Blessed are they who did not see, and yet believed."* The resurrection changed the course of history for anyone who may have doubted who Jesus claimed to be.

Archeological and Historical Findings

A third and unveiling piece of evidence for the Bible's uniqueness is its archeological and historical accuracy. Archeologists consistently uncover new pieces of artifacts that match biblical descriptions. Claims need to be backed up with substantial findings to bring clarity and proof to what would otherwise be seen as speculation. All religious books and materials should be examined with the same dependable tools of research and measurements.

By investigating Christianity and other faiths, I am holding up facts under the light of cross-examination, questioning to find evidence that demands a verdict. Remember that I too was once on the other side, and so were all the skeptics and atheists I mentioned earlier in this book. I hope that by taking time to analyze some of these topics, this book will help individuals dig deeper and search further on their own. My goal is to keep this book concise, so I'm sharing a limited amount of information. It would be helpful to pick up some of the books by the recommended authors, as they can give some solid answers to further questions (Lewis, Strobel, Wallace, McDowell).

It's been said that the Bible is a collection of myths written by ancient Hebrew writers. However, modern technology and archeological findings have given proof otherwise. In Russ Whitten's article "Have You Ever Wondered: Is the Bible historically accurate?" he tells the reader, "There have been thousands of archaeological discoveries in the past century that support every book in the Bible." He explains that misbeliefs, such as "legendary, mythical" characters such as King David, are proven to be reliable and accurate figures of biblical history simply by uncovering evidence through archeological finds.[14]

Many others can give solid evidence that matches the Bible's information geologically, historically, and archeologically. This in turn leads us to the authenticity of the theology of the Bible. Joel P. Kramer, from expeditionbible.com, shares a number of fascinating videos that secure the Bible's veracity. Many of the archaeological artifacts in the Middle East match the description in the Bible and its timeframe. When archaeology began, the Bible was used as a history book and therefore a reference point. But today it's dismissed because of the secular and personal biases of the archaeologists involved. However, they cannot dismiss the puzzle pieces they find that match biblical descriptions.

A key argument for Muslims against the Christian faith is that the Bible has been changed (corrupted) over time. The Old Testament was verified when the Dead Sea scrolls were discovered around 1947, and when those ancient writings were analyzed, they dated from the third century BC to about AD 68. The Qumran community lived in that area and hid them in clay jars as the Roman unrest began to heighten. This fantastic discovery established that the Old Testament scripture wasn't tainted or corrupted. In his article "Has the Bible Been Accurately Copied Down through the Centuries?", Norman Geisler states that comparative studies have shown that the word-for-word identity was in 95% of the Old Testament text. This archeological discovery gives proof of the integrity of the Old Testament. Furthermore, the 5% difference made no fundamental changes when compared to their Hebrew Old Testament.

When the Dead Sea Scrolls' documentation was compared to the Old Testament we have today, it proved to be virtually correct except for a few minor variations. This answered the age-old question regarding the accuracy of the Old Testament. Isn't that incredible! For those who claim that there are so many "errors" in the Bible, it's essential to note that *none* of those minor errors affected the Bible's theology. Minor variant errors were reported in punctuation and spelling, likely due to lighting, eyesight (they couldn't get glasses), or slips of the pen when copying from one document to another. And more importantly, none of these variants would take away from the core of their theology.

We can know that Jesus of Nazareth actually lived. Why? Because separate and apart from people's biases, the biographies of the New Testament writers pass all the known history tests. This includes the internal and external evidence tests and the bibliographical standards used to determine historical and ancient personalities.

The only other more reliable historical book outside the Old Testament is the New Testament. Consider these facts: more manuscripts exist for the New Testament than any other historical book; the original manuscripts of the New Testament are closer in age than any other documents in history; some key eyewitnesses verified and wrote about the death and resurrection of Jesus Christ.[15] And those original writings were written within their lifespan and were not written by others after their deaths. On top of that, these individuals would not deny Jesus, even when they were threatened with martyrdom.

Geisler has studied the accuracy needed to pass historical records and has stated, "The Bible is the most accurately transmitted book from the ancient world. No other ancient book has as many, as early, or more accurately copied manuscripts." The New Testament has proven to be 99.9% accurate.[16]

"In case after case, archeology eventually catches up with the biblical account, and archeology and the Bible come into agreement … Archeology has never proved the biblical account to be wrong, although, in some cases, it lacks the evidence to prove the Biblical account right. As archeologists continue to dig, we will have more and more external evidence to substantiate the historicity and truthfulness of the Bible's record."[17] The Bible has been studied and scrutinized more than any other book. It's been 2000 years since Christ and over 3,500 years since Scripture writings, and it has yet to be falsified. It would be easy to disprove the Bible simply by examining some of its statements. An example could be a town mentioned in a specific place but discovered elsewhere; however, the archeological findings verify the precision of such biblical content. The same tools for examining evidence and reliability could be used for any sacred writings.

In Lee Strobel's book *The Case for Christ,* he states, "although Joseph Smith, the founder of the Mormon church, claimed that his *Book of Mormon* is 'the most correct of any book on earth,' archeology has repeatedly failed to substantiate its claims about events that supposedly occurred long ago in America."[18] Authors John Anderberg and John Weldon give evidence and inform the reader that no archeological work to date has located a Mormon city, person, place, nation, or name, and no artifacts or Book of Mormon scripture or inscriptions have ever been discovered.[19]

When holding up any religious book to the light of examination, we should be able to ask the same series of needed historical and archeological questions to study the evidence. Whether it's the Christian faith or any faith we're investigating, these questions are necessary to show the accuracy of that religious book.

Chapter Nine

BIBLICAL PROPHECY,
BIBLICAL ACCURACY

The fourth and outstanding proof of the Christian faith and the Bible's truth would be the foretelling of things to come—prophecy. God's prophecy in the Bible is so amazing, accurate, and precise that there can be no denying that God Himself wrote this book! It's estimated that about 30% of the Bible is prophecy. That's over a quarter of the Bible! That's a remarkable fact! And it's not just "predictions" but "prophecies," the foretelling that has happened and is now a part of the world's history, with many fulfilled and more to come.

So why aren't more churches teaching future prophecy as part of the Bible? I think there are a number of reasons. Some pastors may feel that this won't attract people to the church, and others may have a hard time deciphering, or perhaps believing, that prophecies could be literal. Yet we've seen Christ fulfill all of them for His first appearance. Sometimes people don't want to know what the future may hold, so they don't want to look at or study it. Remember the ostrich? Wisdom encompasses the study of things past and things to come so that one can make informed decisions.

I believe that future prophecies are not allegorical but literal. And if others would make it worth their study time, they could make an informed decision about who Jesus claimed to be and what the Word says about the future. The evidence of the Messiah's first appearance, and the unveiling of things to come, paint a vivid picture of Christ's future second return. My evaluation of trust begins by seeing the prophecies for Christ's first visitation to earth having been fulfilled with great precision. Based on that information, I don't doubt that everything else prophesied in the Bible will also happen. Isaiah 9:6 says that the government will rest on His shoulders. So what can we make of that?

Strong Pillars to Lean On

There are at least four distinct pillars of Christianity that contrast with other world religions: multiple writers as opposed to one person's vision, with a consistent thread written over the span of 1,500 years; the resurrection; the archeological and historical evidence; and the precision of the prophecies.

The Bible has *never* been wrong in the prophecies given to date, and they have taken place exactly and precisely as predicted in Scripture. Biblical prophecy shows that the Bible is accurate and that it could only be authored by God, not man. In 2 Peter 1:20–21, we're told how the prophecies came into being:

> But know this first of all, that no prophecy of Scripture becomes a matter of someone's own interpretation, for no prophecy was ever made by an act of human will, but men moved by the Holy Spirit spoke from God.

Prophecies about the Messiah had been foretold over three hundred times throughout the Bible. They were repeated in different ways through different writers that point directly to the Jewish Messiah—Jesus. All the foretelling prophecies have been fulfilled for Jesus' first arrival, with future prophecies to be fulfilled following the rapture and before His second arrival. This divine foretelling speaks both of a suffering Servant and a reigning King. The reigning King is yet to come.

Prophecy is one of the best proofs to showcase our God, and it's one of the main pillars that distinguish Christianity from other world religions. Only God knows the future and can reveal accurate details of future events. Do other religions have prophecy? Do they give dates, times, and events, or is it just general statements? Have any come to pass? There is no possible way that humans can predict what the Bible predicts. It tells us of world powers before they happen and history before it exists. It's incredible! The fact that hundreds of specific prophecies are now a part of our history should really wake us up, and in case we get sleepy, get out the smelling salts!

---

*Biblical prophecy shows that the Bible is
accurate and that it could only be authored
by God, not man.*

Newsworthy

Although it's never heralded from the newsstands, hundreds of biblical prophecies have been fulfilled, which include many other prophecies outside of the Jewish Messiah's arrival. The Bible also talks about empires, such as Alexander the Great's, long before they ever existed. Accurate and precise, it remains remarkable to me that this is never publicized on mainstream media. Instead, the Bible, God, and followers of Jesus are ridiculed and mocked because the god of media speaks—and sadly, people listen. The Christian faith is slanted to look dumbed down and foolish in the eyes of the world.

Our media rules, and Christians are often mocked and ridiculed on a variety of platforms. But why does that surprise us? If it's truth and light to the world, then the Judeo-Christian principles will be attacked because they *are* just that—God's truth.

The media describes Christians as fools, but God also talks about fools. It isn't the believers who are considered fools in His eyes but those who do not or will not take the time to seek Him and find out that He seeks them too: "*The fool has said in his heart, 'There is no God'*" (Psalm 14:1a).

I have never seen a magazine at the cash-out announcing, "Hundreds of Biblical Prophecies Come True with Great Accuracy and Precision!" with the subtitle, "Read and Study Them All—Just to

See What an Amazing God We Have!" Yet individuals will pick up and read, with great intrigue, the most absurd of all stories and believe them. The world went crazy with the Mayan calendar pointing to the end of it all. That ancient cult gave human sacrifices to their gods. Why would we even look twice at that? But the whole world did, and they were biting their nails as the clock ticked. Yet God speaks, and the world does not listen. In fact, it puts in earplugs!

Precision and Accuracy

Do we take the time to study, meditate, or read God's Word to find out what He says about His time schedule or calendar? Yet His accuracy has been 100% precise to date.

Prophecies were also given in the Bible about events besides Jesus' coming. Some are events yet to come, some are history, and others are a foretelling to bring hope at an appointed time. One example is the seventy years the Jewish people would be exiled in Babylon. The Israelites became an evil people throughout their land, and God gave them plenty of time and methods of discipline to help guide them back on track. They deliberately refused, and then He handed them over to the Babylonians. However, there was a remnant of a few faithful followers, and Daniel was one of them.

Daniel held on to a promise recorded in Jeremiah 29:10: "*For this is what the Lord says: 'When seventy years have been completed for Babylon, i will visit you and fulfill my good word to you, to bring you back to this place.'*" He hung on to those prophetic words as God's promise to His people while he and the other Jewish captives were in Babylon. He believed God would rescue His people after the seventy years because of the above prophecy, and he counted down the calendar until it was so. The rebuilding of their Jewish temple, the return of the Hebrew people, the repair of Jerusalem, the Jewish hearts rendering back to their God (after seventy years of exile in Babylon) are recorded in the books of Ezra and Nehemiah. They are precisely what God said would come to pass. Dozens of prophecies were fulfilled in this story alone.

It was also the prophet Daniel who spoke to King Nebuchadnezzar about the vision the king had in his dream. Because Daniel was able to tell and interpret it for him, he spared many a prophet and soothsayer their heads! I'm sure those soothsayers pulled out a banner, stamped "HERO" in capital letters, and then painted Daniel's picture beside it!

Is Alexander the Great's Empire in the Bible?

The book of Daniel includes some amazing historical facts that were written well before any of them came into being, and they determined political powers and position before they occurred. The Bible doesn't use the name of Alexander the Great, but it certainly tells about his empire. And the Greek Empire was more influential in spreading the gospel than you may realize!

Biblical and ancient history record King Nebuchadnezzar's rule during the Neo-Babylonian Empire. Following that was the rise and fall of the empires and kingdoms. The Bible and history pages give us a match! They are recorded in the book of Daniel and have taken place in the exact order that history has shown us. Some of it is history and has already happened, and some of the events in the book of Daniel are future events.

In Daniel 2, Daniel interprets King "Nebby's" dream. The Babylonian ruler had no compassion. He wanted his soothsayers to both tell him his dream and describe what it meant. When they couldn't, Daniel came in to save the day. He prayed to God, and He delivered. The dream was of a giant statue that represented four kingdoms during and following the king's reign: first Babylon, then Medo-Persia, followed by Greece (Alexander), and then Rome. The head was made of pure gold, which would be Babylonia; its chest and two arms were in silver, representing two kingdoms—the Medes and the Persians (Medo-Persia). Then we have its belly and thighs made of bronze—the Greeks; and legs of iron, its feet partly of iron and partly of clay—the Roman Empire but also a revised Roman Empire yet to come, a future prophecy yet to be fulfilled.[20]

In Daniel 2, Daniel explains to the king that after his kingdom, another will arise that will be inferior to the Babylonian Kingdom. This will be followed by a third and powerful kingdom, described as bronze—the Greeks with Alexander at the helm. The legendary conquests of Alexander took over most of the world, and the Greek language became the common universal language.

Daniel continues to describe the fourth kingdom as being strong as iron, breaking and smashing everything else. As we know, the Roman Empire did just that and covered most of the land mass of the then-known world.

The Medo-Persian and the Greek take-over are discussed in Daniel 8:20–22, but the remaining passages of Daniel 8 tell of a time yet to come. We see a more detailed view of Medo-Persia and the conquest of Alexander the Great over them: "*Then the male goat made himself exceedingly great. But once he became powerful, the large horn was broken; and in its place four prominent horns ...*" (Daniel 8:8). This was written around 500 BC, two centuries before the events that took place in approximately 300 BC, in the exact order and time needed to fulfill history. The goat coming out of the west would represent Alexander's rule over the earth, which dies along with Alexander when he meets his untimely death at thirty-two years of age.[21]

We see in Daniel 8:20–21 the breakdown of the Greek Empire, which gets divided among his four Greek generals and not blood relatives. That is exactly what happened; after Alexander's death, the Greek Empire was divided among his four generals. From there, it goes to two stronger generals, which became the Seleucid and Ptolemaic Empires. When the Roman Empire arrived on the scene, it became the fulfillment of time for the Jewish Messiah's arrival (Galatians 4:4). Some mathematicians say that the odds of this prophecy alone being fulfilled are astronomical. Who can predict the future so precisely? Only God Himself.

The Roman and Greek Empires were prominent catalysts to Christ's and the apostles' mission and helped to spread the gospel in a quick and efficient manner. Once Alexander conquered most of the world, Greek became the common language, known as Koine Greek, and was used by the common folk. The posh Greek scholars and philosophers used a different dialect. Later the Old Testament would be translated into Greek, and that became known as the Septuagint. So this common Greek dialect was spoken far and wide, and the Bible was written in Koine Greek. Having a common language running through the Roman Empire made it easy to teach and preach without learning the individual foreign languages.

Another interesting tidbit concerns the Roman roads. Long before Jesus' day, the Roman roads were designed and built to last! Some still exist today! On the other hand, my city has roads that crumble yearly, and we have potholes that can swallow a car! We could use some Roman insight into road building! Arrgghhh! Okay ... I'm better now. At the height of the Roman Empire, there were about 250,000 miles of road and approximately 50,000 miles of highway. The roads branched out from Rome (hence the saying "all roads lead to Rome") and radiated into highways going into many territories. That established the most accessible form of travel and gave quick access to other provinces and cities. This was extended throughout all the Roman-occupied land. The Roman and the Greek Empires worked together to become the perfect time for Christ and the apostles to take the gospel to their world, with one common language and travel-worthy roads.

The prophetic book of Daniel speaks of future prophecies as well. They point to an end-time ruler from a revived Roman Empire, and we're told more about that in Daniel 7 and 8. In his book *The Non-Prophets Guide to the Book of Revelation,* Todd Hampson explains how symbolism is used in these prophetic books of the Bible: "Whenever a symbol is used in Revelation, we must do a bit of homework to see how it is used elsewhere in Scripture. We don't get to pick and decide for ourselves the meaning of the symbols."[22]

In Hampson's easy-to-understand format, he explains many things that were once foggy to me. The books of Daniel and Revelation are, in my estimation, the two most challenging books of the Bible and go hand in hand with unfolding future prophecies. So although these prophecies may appear to be like hieroglyphics, it's not impossible to uncover some of the mysteries; it just takes a little work.

The Bible can be simple if we just want to accept the good news through Jesus Christ, or it can become a lifetime study book. The Old Testament prophets would never have been able to decipher what they were writing, but it all came to pass, with Jesus arriving at the appointed time. Because of this, I believe the future prophecies are literal and will come to pass, as they did in the past.

The Impossibility of Probability—Unless There Is a God

Let's look at the probability of just a few biblical prophecies taking place as God said they would. Dr. Peter Stoner (1888–1980) was both a science professor at Westmount College and a mathematics and astronomy professor at Pasadena City College. The American Science Affiliation verified his findings outlined below. Dr. Stoner, along with six hundred students, decided to check into the odds of probability with a few of the prophecies that Christ fulfilled. Out of all the Messianic prophecies foretold, Dr. Stoner took just eight of the historically-fulfilled prophecies of Jesus and worked out the mathematical odds of that small handful alone.[23]

Here was the kicker for me—if you took *only eight* of the historically-proven prophecies, the impossibility of that would be 10 to the 17th power. Do you know what that looks like? Here it is: 100,000,000,000,000,000. Wow! Can you name that number without looking it up? That's only a handful of the Old Testament prophecies that Jesus fulfilled, yet dozens more have taken place. There is no way that this is humanly possible unless God is involved.

To give you a visual, this would be like taking enough $1 American silver coins and marking only *one* of them with an X. Now lay the coins end to end and two-feet deep through the entire state of Texas, with the X coin anywhere in the entire state. Following that, allow one person only one chance to go through the entire state and pick out one coin from all directions. What would be the odds of that person picking out that X coin? It would be 10 to the power of 17. Yet Jesus fulfilled those eight prophecies and so many more during His first advent. This can only take place through the hands of God!

No other religion can claim more than a few prophecies in their writings, and certainly none with a timeline with such great clarity as the Word of God. Holding up this measurement for comparison helps us understand why the Bible is so unique. The prophecies for Jesus' first coming have all been fulfilled. We're now seeing the "birth pangs" mentioned in Matthew 24, before Jesus comes again.

The Arrival Time of the Messiah

While writing this section on the arrival time of the Messiah, I'm taking a moment to be grateful that I can lean on the knowledge of other researchers and authors who have discovered these facts. They have invested so much time and devotion, and bring years of knowledge and research to light. We're fortunate to glean from their wisdom. Much of this knowledge, artifacts found, and unearthed discoveries have taken place in the last century and are evidence that God wants to be known by you and has made Himself available to be found!

As I researched various topics, I found that many scholars and teachers give differing years for historical dates. Some believe that Nebuchadnezzar conquered Jerusalem in either 587 or 586 BC, or that the Dead Sea scrolls were found in either 1948 or 1947. However, it's important to realize that this doesn't change the fact that it happened. Other things, such as a year when the king took over a reign, may differ, and so it is when trying to decipher times of decrees. Although there are different variables, we can still confidently say that Jesus', the Messiah's, time of arrival was met!

The Messiah had hundreds of prophecies that needed to be fulfilled. I want to cover just a handful of prophecies before we move on. Keep in mind that Christ fulfilled *all* the prophecies for His first coming recorded in the Old Testament. Let's take a look at just a few mentioned in the Word:

- His virgin birth was recorded seven hundred years before it came to be. In Isaiah 7:14, we read, "*Therefore the Lord Himself will give you a sign: Behold, the virgin will conceive and give birth to a son, and she will name Him Immanuel.*"
- Jesus' birthplace in Bethlehem Ephrathah is exceptionally timely because it wasn't even Mary and Joseph's hometown. They travelled for a census and gave birth in Bethlehem (there were two Bethlehems in the region, so it's specific), which had been written about seven hundred years earlier in Micah 5:2: "*But you, Bethlehem Ephrathah, though you are little among the thousands of Judah, yet out of you shall come forth to Me the One to be Ruler in Israel, Whose goings forth are from old, from everlasting*" (NKJV).
- Being born into the line of King David (Isaiah 9:7; Jeremiah 23:5).
- Being betrayed by a friend (Judas) (Psalm 41:9, 55:12–14).
- Being sold for thirty pieces of silver and the money being thrown down to go to the potter's field (Zechariah 11:12–13).
- Soldiers at the cross gambling for His clothing (Psalm 22:18).
- Dying for our transgressions between two criminals (Isaiah 53:12).
- His body being pierced on the cross, both with a spear and pierced hands and feet (Zechariah 12:10; Psalm 22:16).
- His death by crucifixion (Psalm 22).

The above prophecies have been proven historically, and the remaining prophecies yet to be fulfilled will happen during what the Bible calls the Tribulation time and the Messiah's Second Coming to earth. Before Christ returns a second time, both the Jewish people and Israel were to fulfill some prophecies. Those prophecies were completed when Israel became a nation in 1948.

The arrival schedule of the Jewish Messiah (first advent) is so profound that it's almost unbelievable! Had it not been proven historically, it would be hard to believe. Looking at Daniel 9:24–26 requires some insight into the prophecies and the Jewish calendar, but it gives us the exact period of time, the appointed time, of Jesus' arrival on earth to fulfill His purpose and mission.

For many years now, as I study the Word, I am noticing world events lining up with scripture. Eschatology may be an uncomfortable subject to study, but it's crucial to know the times. We can be prepared. A number of Bible scholars study a 490-year calendar for both Christ's first and second arrival to earth.

God uses certain numbers to accomplish His works. Seven is significant and reveals that something is completed, finished, or perfected. He created seven days in one week and gave the Jewish people a command to let their land rest on the seventh year, called a Shemitah year. Joshua was told to march around Jericho seven times. There's more, but you get the picture. Even our secular world has a "lucky seven." Hmm ... I wonder if they know who's behind that?

The prophecy of the Jewish Messiah's first arrival is given to us in the book of Daniel and takes a bit of explaining to understand, but it is so do-able! Let's start with the scripture in Daniel 9:24–26, where God's angel messenger Gabriel informs Daniel about the Jewish Messiah's first arrival and gives a timeline of when He would die. Following that, he informs Daniel of the Messiah's second arrival to the world:

*Seventy weeks have been decreed for your people and your holy city,
to finish the wrongdoing, to make an end of sin, to make atonement
for guilt, to bring in everlasting righteousness, to seal up vision and
prophecy, and to anoint the Most Holy Place. So you are to know
and understand that from the issuing of a decree to restore and rebuild
Jerusalem, until Messiah the Prince, there will be seven weeks and
sixty-two weeks; it will be built again, with streets and moat, even
in times of distress. Then after sixty-two weeks, the Messiah will be
cut off and have nothing, and the people of the prince who is to come
will destroy the city and the sanctuary ...*

In other Bible versions, verse 24 begins with, "Seventy 'sevens.'"
I'm going to go with that easier version to help with comprehension.
In order to give all the information, a deeper study would be needed.
For all the essential details to be examined, note the authors mentioned in the endnotes for this chapter. For now, I'm explaining in a
simple format, which may seem like a wide brush stroke (and is), but
it gives the broad picture. The seven "weeks" are actually years, the
total number of years decreed to complete the prophetic calendar—
which multiplied by seven, or "seventy sevens," equals 490 years. A
490-year prophetic calendar is used for the countdown to the Jewish
Messiah's arrivals on earth, with 483 years being His first, and 7 more
years until He returns a second time.

After His first arrival, there's an undisclosed period of time
known as the "Church Age," which is the period of time when the
Church of believers is on the earth before rapture. It's like the clock
has paused during this moment in time. After the rapture, the calendar continues and heads toward the end-time prophecy. At the end of
the seven-year Tribulation period (I will discuss the Rapture, Church
Age, and the Tribulation in a future chapter), the second arrival of
Jesus to earth will happen, also known as the Second Coming (or second advent).

The Tribulation period is seven years long, and then Jesus returns to earth. In between the 483 years and the 7-year tribulation period (483 + 7 = 490) is an undisclosed amount of time, called the Church Age, which started after Christ's resurrection, on the day of Pentecost to be exact, and will continue until the rapture of believers in Christ.

The "seven weeks and sixty-two weeks" can be broken down as: 7 "weeks" (years) x 7 = 49 years, and 62 "weeks" (years) x 7 = 434 years. Together they equal 483 years. To continue, it will be helpful to break this down into three parts.

The first portion would be a period of forty-nine years. The time it is said to have taken to complete the rebuilding of the temple once it was destroyed by the Babylonians.

Before their Babylonian captivity, the Jewish people became extremely wicked. For many centuries, God warned, disciplined, and showed them the way out of their sorry mess, but they refused. At that time in Jerusalem, they still had Solomon's temple to worship and hold sacrifices to God, but few were in right standing with God. Daniel was one of the few. Then the Babylonians took over and destroyed both Jerusalem and the temple around 586 BC, taking the Jewish people captive. They enslaved the Hebrew people for seventy years, and some prominent figures were released to begin the process of rebuilding their temple so that they could prepare and begin serving their God. Nothing was easy, and much of the building process flat-lined for decades. A number of decrees were given by the different Persian kings as the building process was constantly halted by opposers, giving hardship to those involved. The first set of sevens is the length of time it took to rebuild the temple, which was held up by political unrest or *even in times of distress.*

Before we move on to the other two portions of the 490-year calendar, it's important to explain that decrees from various kings were issued for many years to rebuild the temple, and also for financing the Jewish sacrifices. But the total restoration and rebuilding process of Jerusalem (restore and rebuild) was never completed until the final rebuilding decree was given through King Artaxerxes. This completed the rebuilding of the walls against enemy attack, finally bringing needed restoration to the people and their faith. Artaxerxes' first decree is said to have been dated as either 458 or 457 BC, but things were still delayed. His second decree has been dated in either 445 or 444 BC. The total restoration of the city of Jerusalem and the rebuilding of the walls were completed under the Persian king, Artaxerxes. The rebuilding is recorded in the books of Ezra and Nehemiah.

The second portion would be a period of 434 years. "*So you are to know and understand that from the issuing of a decree to restore and rebuild Jerusalem, until Messiah the Prince, there will be seven weeks and sixty-two weeks ...*" (Daniel 9:25). This verse separates the seven weeks and the sixty-two weeks so that we are aware of the first event. The next amount was 62 years x 7, or 434 years. The 49 years + 434 years = 483 years. At the end of the 483 years, the Jewish Messiah will be put to death. This gives us the precise time period in which the Messiah needed to be on earth to complete His purpose and mission, which would be 483 years (49 + 434 = 483) after the decree and when the Anointed One would be cut off (killed) "but not for Himself." This would have to happen before the destruction of the rebuilt (and later refurbished by Herod the Great) second temple that was completed through the decree of Artaxerxes. And that Jewish temple (considered as the second temple) was destroyed by the Romans in AD 70, completing Daniel 9:26.

The ancient Jewish lunar calendar seems to have come from their Babylonian captivity. So there is a 360-day count for their calendar year, which is also called a prophetic calendar year. However, others have used the solar calendar, and it still gives us the period of time when Jesus walked the earth and was crucified. Through various studies I have seen different dates given for Jesus' birth and therefore His death. However, we can be confidant that His crucifixion happened in the 1st century, AND before the second temple was destroyed. We know according to Daniel 9:25–26 that the Anointed One (the

Messiah) will be put to death before the destruction of the city and the sanctuary (or temple) caused by the Romans in AD 70. That's exactly what happened!

Looking at Artaxerxes last decree of 445-444 BC and adding the 483 years of the 360 lunar calendar brings us to Christ's duration on earth, fulfilled prophecies, and His crucifixion, all before the destruction of the city and the temple by the Romans in AD 70!

There are other prophecies that pointed to the Messiah being on earth while the temple was still standing and before the destruction of it and the city of Jerusalem by the Romans in AD 70; they are Malachi 3:1, Psalm 118:26, and Genesis 49:10. By this we know that the Messiah had to arrive in the first century before the temple was destroyed by the Romans, and to date, it has not been rebuilt.

This type of knowledge helps us know just how remarkable our God is! The first time I heard this, I was both shaking my head and picking my jaw up off the floor! God has outdone Himself. Such revelation knowledge is almost too much to comprehend and should cause us to simply worship Him! Why would God take the time to uncover these discoveries for us to see? Because He wants us to know and reverence Him. When we gather facts such as these, it strengthens us and gives us evidence and the resiliency to desire to know more about our God and Saviour.

On Palm Sunday, the crowds shouted praises and gave honour to their Messiah. In Matthew 21, we're told of their worship as they exclaimed, "*Hosanna to the Son of David; blessed is the One who comes in the name of the Lord; Hosanna in the highest!*" These statements were quoted from the Old Testament in Psalm 118:25, acknowledging and praising Jesus as the Messiah, with "Hosanna" being shouted, meaning "save (deliver) us." What the crowd didn't realize was that this wasn't the moment for Him to set up the kingdom. That was yet to come. At that time, they were expecting their warrior Messiah to begin taking care of business with the Romans. They were unaware that He needed to fulfill the prophecy of the suffering Servant (Isaiah 53; Psalm 22;

Luke 19:10, 11). Even though that was in their Scripture as well, they were ignorant, and many turned their backs on Him in a few short days. He didn't give them what they came to seek Him for, and many turned on Him and yelled for Him to be crucified.

The third and final part of this prophecy is a period of one "week" or seven years (1 year X 7 = 7 years). This is called the Tribulation Period, which is yet to come (Daniel 9:27). So we have the three periods of time: 49+434+7= 490 years, completing the 490-year prophetic calendar.[24]

Centuries ago, readers of the Bible couldn't foresee how those curious prophecies would come to pass. Yet today it's crystal clear. In rapid succession, many world events have taken a position on the world stage. Almost all of it is out in full view, so one can't use the term "conspiracy" and point fingers. Conspiracy denotes something being theoretical, but if the media lets us in on future plans, and the evidence closes in on us daily, one can no longer call it a conspiracy.

Today I see that we could have torn a few pages out of Ray Bradbury's 1953 science fiction novel *Fahrenheit 451*. The parallels are uncanny and pull up close beside our reality. It's hard to imagine that it was written seventy years ago. There are even robot dogs in Bradbury's book, and if you check out the artificial metal dogs being created today, it's easy to see how technology has taken us to this place and is rapidly beginning to substitute all things with a heartbeat.

Technology takeover has replaced human relationships in multiple ways. Many people have turned to high tech for almost everything. Virtual reality has replaced human connection and what God has created humankind for—fellowship and love for one another in personal relationships and with Him. I recently heard a story of a distraught father asking his pastor for help and prayer over his suicidal teenage boy. This teenager had fallen in love with a virtual-reality woman and knew he could never have her. Because she wasn't real, he couldn't have her in his real world, so the young man became so distraught that he felt he couldn't live without her.

This is just the tiniest tip of the iceberg. We're seeing events unfold that are the markers of future prophecies. If all the signs have already been fulfilled in the past, then we can count on the future ones also coming to pass. By far the most prominent marker would be being globally connected. In the last few decades, technology has moved in unprecedented ways to globally connect us. These signposts make us aware that something is shifting in our world: others having the capacity to control our lives, supply chains getting choked out, advanced technology taking over—not only through a lack of human contact but also replacing human jobs, and artificial intelligence replacing human intelligence, etc. There is a strong movement toward the world's economies using digital currency only, and it seems like the Great Reset button is getting ready to be pushed (check out *Time International*'s cover, "The Great Reset," October 23, 2020), with a host of other examples indicating future change. What would have appeared to be a strange mystery to the readers of the Word centuries ago has now transpired before our very eyes. The believers of the past couldn't foresee what the unveiling of the future would look like, yet they still held the Bible as the truth they stood on. They were people of great faith.

Chapter Ten

WHAT ABOUT HYPOCRISY?

Hypocrisy is an important topic. In fact, hypocrites may be the very reason why many people don't search out the Christian faith. There are hypocrites in every arena of life, but the world shines a spotlight on those claiming to be Christ-believers. Some individuals say that churches and faith-filled people are hypocrites, and if that's your viewpoint, you're right!

Hypocrites and the Church

There are those who use hypocrites to justify their refusal to check out Christianity. But if we look closer, we'll find that no one in this world is without hypocrisy; in fact, it's impossible to be human and be without hypocrisy. There was only *One* who walked this earth who was not a hypocrite, and He was without sin (1 Peter 2:22; 1 John 3:5; Hebrews 4:15).

I will stand up and say that I am a hypocrite, but if you look in the mirror, you'll see one too. Humans are flawed with a sinful nature. We all live with regrets. Hurt people hurt people. It makes logical sense that if we as humans are sinners, we need someone sinless to take our place, as we can never be good enough on our own merit, *because* we are hypocrites. It's about God reaching down to us, not us reaching up to Him.

The Bible says about all of humanity that *"There is no righteous person, not even one"* (Romans 3:10). According to this verse, no one is without hypocrisy. I once heard a sermon that helped me rephrase the word "hypocrite" to "sinner." You may reason that you don't go to church or believe in Christ because of the hypocrites. In that case, it may be helpful for you to look at that hypocrite (sinner) as being another person going to the hospital (church) to get a weekly blood transfusion (spiritual boost).

We're all hypocrites. There will be no excuse or pointing fingers at another person one day when we individually meet God, because it never was about "them"; it has always been about you and Him. None of us is righteous in and of ourselves, but we can choose to wear the robe of righteousness through Christ Jesus. It pains me to re-examine my life and see how I too have failed on many levels, but He is a forgiver, and we can start anew today. My pastor for many years, Pastor Leon, often said, "I am not where I want to be, but thank God, I am not where I used to be."

You can fill in the blanks. "I am not a good Christian when …" For myself, I'm not a good Christian when I'm overtired, overstressed, overworked, or overwhelmed—yep, that about covers it! There are days that I'd like to turn back the hands of times and redo things in my life. Many times it feels like I'm mopping up the mess of my past, and I wish I could have left fewer puddles and just done better. Regrets have a way of chasing and catching up to us as we get older. On the other hand, I can't imagine the path I'd have taken without Jesus. One day, Ruth Bell Graham, wife of evangelist Billy Graham, drove through a construction zone and decided upon the epitaph she wanted on her tombstone. When she was laid to rest, she did indeed have that saying carved into her stone: "End of construction. Thank you for your patience." I think each of us can echo that statement.

We're all hypocrites in the sense of being sinners, and we may even be a struggling Christian with habits or attitudes that we dislike, but His followers will come back to Him, confess, and get right before God. That's what made King David a man after God's own heart. He blew it with bloodshed and adultery on his hands, but his heart consistently and consciously turned back to God. King David repented to be in right standing before God. This doesn't mean King David didn't suffer the consequences of his actions, but he knew that the quickest detour was to turn and fast-track back to His Father and then get in right standing before Him as soon as possible.

People have been hurt by a specific person in a church or by the church itself. They've attached the word "Jesus" to the mistreatment of others in history. There have been false teachers, preachers, and churches that have stood for centuries and created some very ugly scenes in church history, causing many to say, "If this is faith, I don't want it." However, it was people who perverted the faith, not Jesus. And that is where the tables turn!

I could write chapters on hypocrisy and church history. It hurts me and others to see how badly some churches (who professed to be Christian churches) could hate so profoundly and hurt others so badly. We can't even imagine how much it must hurt God! The bottom line is that God never taught us to force someone into a faith, whether Christian or Muslim, Protestant or Catholic. Even God gave the angels free will to serve Him or not. Free will is essential for authentic love because forced love is no love at all. Jesus died for all humankind and even cared about those who nailed Him to the cross (Luke 23:34). He was love and forgiveness, not hate and forcefulness.

When I think of these horrific events of church history, I think of the attributes of Jesus and have questioned if this is what Jesus would do. Then I go back to the Bible, where in Mark 6:11 Jesus tells the disciples to "*... shake the dust off your feet as a testimony against them.*" When someone didn't want to hear about the offer of freedom from their sin through the grace of the gospel, the disciples were to shake the dust off their feet, and that individual's testimony would be held against them when they faced God one day. However, with prayer and love we may have future opportunities to instill the gospel to these individuals once again. There is hope. God can move through the power of prayer.

He has made a way, and He has provided for those who want Him in their life. So perhaps we can change the question from "Why would a loving God send anyone to Hell?" to "Why would anyone reject a loving God's gift of salvation?"

---

*Free will is essential for authentic love because
forced love is no love at all.*

Pride

Pride is so debilitating. It's the chief sin that destroys humanity and causes many of us not to acknowledge God and Christ. Even the angels had free will (Isaiah 14:12–15), and pride brought down one-third of them from Heaven. Pride is far more hidden and subtle than struggles with things like addictions and behaviours. However, pride is far more likely to knock us off track in seeking God. It blocks us from getting to know Him. It disables us from bowing a knee, and it enables us to continue in our own way. First John 2:16 says, "*For all that is in the world, the lust of the flesh and the lust of the eyes and the boastful pride of life, is not from the Father, but is from the world.*"

Without God and His gift of salvation, what kind of hope do we have for humankind's sinful nature? I'm sure you can answer that one. People are turning on each other because they're looking to themselves and others instead of to the Father. If we observe others through God's lens, we view them differently. When we gaze through the lens of God's mercy and grace, it helps us to view others with His love. Each of us would do well to remember whom we have placed in the driver's seat of our lives. When you look in the mirror, remember that He created you, and when you look in the rear-view mirror, remember that He created them!

The Bible is clear about meeting God on Judgement Day and about those who say they are Christians but clearly are not: "*Not everyone who says to Me, 'Lord, Lord,' will enter the kingdom of heaven …*" (Matthew 7:21). According to this verse, we can use all the correct Christian-ese terms and still not have a heart for Jesus. We can't fool

Him. The people in Matthew 7:21 did their own thing. These could be false evangelists, deceptive leaders, and others who may fool people, but they can't fool God. They don't care about repentance or what God's Word has to say, yet they claim to be Christians. So there is no need to look at those who are hypocrites in your eyes; God knows who they are. Our business is to look inward and then upwards to Him.

We can choose to ignore Him, but He won't go away. In the end, we will meet Him face to face (Romans 14:10–11; 2 Corinthians 5:10), and we will answer for ourselves. In Philippians 2:10–11, Paul says:

> *so that at the name of Jesus every knee will bow, of those who are in heaven and on earth and under the earth, and that every tongue will confess that Jesus Christ is Lord, to the glory of God the Father.*

Whether one believes it or not, the Bible tells us that there will be a day when everyone will acknowledge Jesus as Lord.

Chapter Eleven

TRANSFORMATION

Reflecting on a personal faith and decision for Jesus Christ requires humility and wisdom. Who did He claim to be, who do we believe Him to be, and what do we do with that? An act of your will and volition is involved in this relationship, just like any other healthy relationship. Evidence will not move you if you choose not to be moved.

Evidence for Me

I needed answers before I could walk into a position of accepting Christ as my Saviour. I went to church, met with Christians, and had multiple questions answered before I felt comfortable enough to make a personal commitment to follow Jesus. I moved from traditional church attendance to choosing to trust and have a relationship with Jesus Christ. After I invited Him in, I took the steps needed for my personal growth and began asking a lot of questions. Then as I began researching, the evidence seemed to uncover itself. The answers appeared to rise to the surface. Some people believe that they need to change or become a better person before accepting Jesus. I didn't clean myself up before I received Him—I received Him so He could clean me up!

Many things moved me from a place of intellectual debate to a stance of faith. Evidence convinced me of some needed proof, but I loved the stories of transformed lives. Those transformations show a heart change. I'd like to be further than I am in my knowledge and faith journey. However, as long as I keep studying and inviting the

Holy Spirit in, the transformation continues. In hearing the stories of others, I grow as well. Sometimes growth comes through times of pain, and we don't always see the hand of God move when we're in distress. However, God can cause all things to work together for the good, even though it may not feel like it during those moments, for those who love God and are called according to His purpose (Romans 8:28). Jesus' mother, Mary, must have felt the same way in her moments of anguish.

Mary was at the cross with Jesus according to multiple accounts. She knew who He was. The angel had visited her when she was a young girl and told her—the Saviour of the world. If He truly wasn't the Saviour of the world, any mother in her correct state of mind would try to stop the actions of the Roman soldiers. She would have run up to those who whipped, beat, and nailed her son to the cross and begged and pleaded with them. If He wasn't the Messiah, she would have told them that her son was crazy to have said and done the things He did. She would be pleading for His life. Even if the soldiers didn't listen, she would have tried. But she didn't. She stood by and watched. She watched in deep, sorrowful anguish, and she mourned as she saw Him suffer and die. I can't even imagine that type of a breaking of a parent's heart. This woman did not try to save her son. She stood back and watched Him suffer greatly as He accomplished His mission. To the point of her utter despair and heartbreak, she watched His agony and death, because she knew who He was and why He came to earth.

Life is pain because we live in a broken and fallen world. Jesus said that in this world you will have trouble (John 16:33). That's when we need to trust Him and His promises. Mother Mary's story is one example that not all things *are* good but that they can work together for the good as promised to us in Romans 8:28. As long as we're on this side of Heaven, there will be pain, but He promises to see us through.

Transformed lives give credible testimony of how Jesus can move in people's hearts and make something beautiful out of a messy, no-way-out situation, to creating one of hope. Transformed lives are key to seeing how Jesus can work from the inside out. We all have dark times, and each person has a story. My story involves deep hurt through the infidelity of my first husband, and because God and I have forgiven the individuals involved, I will leave that as enough of an account. The reformation and transformation for those involved comes from the same God who extends grace and mercy to me in my failings. The same redeeming love that forgave them forgives me. The story is really about how the healing took place. God can indeed bind shattered, broken, and messy lives that result from pain. He is a God of restoration. And although the picture may not look exactly the same, He can take the fractured pieces and construct a new picture that can only be explained by letting His hand move on our behalf. The construction process will leave a different but new portrait. And if allowed, He will craft the old pieces into a restored one designed by the Master Artist.

In my darkest hours, and even when I couldn't feel Him, He showed up. In fact, He showed up in so many ways that I'd have to write another book to outline them all. It wasn't about feelings, though—it was about placing my trust in Him, even when I couldn't sense His presence, which seemed to be often at that time. The acuteness of pain has a way of manifesting itself so greatly that everything else seems dulled.

It wasn't immediate, nor was it through a vision given to me that He made Himself evident. I just cried and prayed. That's it—cried and prayed. Most of the time, I just cried, and that became my prayer. This pain moved from days to weeks to months to years. I cried for two years off and on—more on than off—and that became my prayer. I cried, and He heard. At work, I went into the back room to cry and then came out and served the public with glassy eyes. I cried when the children weren't looking and sometimes when they were. In the middle of the night, I woke up, grabbed a towel, and went inside my car and wept till the towel was soaked. In the silence of the night, not wanting to wake the children, the garage became the only option. Then I'd go to sleep (if I could), wake up, go to work, and do it all over again, for a solid two years. That's a lot of crying for someone who rarely cried up to that point. And then I just continued to put one foot in front of the other and paced a day at a time.

God knew my heart couldn't even pray at that time in my life, so I just knelt by my bed and wept instead.

Now in the same way the Spirit also helps our weakness; for we do not know what to pray for as we should, but the Spirit Himself intercedes for us with groanings too deep for words; and He who searches the hearts knows what the mind of the Spirit is, because He intercedes for the saints in accordance with the will of God.
—Romans 8:26–27

Through the tears and even though no words were spoken, my God saw me and heard me, and His Spirit took over to intercede in prayer for me. My submission of bowing down in prayer, with tears and no words, became the act that was still worship to God. Submission is a verb, and it requires a willful heart. God can still hear the heart even when the mouth can't send out a prayer.

This faith wasn't based on a feeling because there was nothing but sorrow at that time. Instead, it was based on the promises in the Word of God, which helped anchor me and let me trust that He was there. He had proved Himself faithful in the past, and I had to trust in that to go forward. In my grief, anguish, and despair, coupled with my pressing into Him, He became more real to me than I could imagine. Time was involved. Then I began receiving more answers to start sorting out my life. I began writing down my frustrations and prayers, then answers to those prayers, and slowly moved into a new place of faith. The more I cried out to Him and sought Him, the more He made Himself known. It wasn't instant, but it was consistent. If I felt anxious at any point in time or had a massive lack of faith, I'd go back to my journal to confirm past answers to prayer and hold on to the affirmation that He would indeed answer again.

It took about a decade to completely heal. A twenty-year marriage and a broken trust (when one trusts so deeply) takes time to heal from. And scars remain. Sin, even sin of another, has ripple effects that affect surrounding lives. It wasn't simple or fast, but I saw the hand of God move in my life. To be sure, God can show up immediately, but that's His choice and for His good reasons. Some people demand that God show up for them and prove Himself to them, but if we know the Word well enough, we know that's not how He usually operates. However, He does show up for some, but He chooses who, and He knows the "why." We don't have to figure it out. God calls us to seek Him, and that act alone proves our sincerity in wanting to know Him. Being on my knees, and with tears for my prayers, became my act of submission and trust.

Satan tempted Jesus in the desert, telling Him to defy the laws of gravity. Jesus quoted the Word: "*You shall not put the Lord your God to the test*" (Matthew 4:7b). We are not to test God but to move by faith and not by sight. We are not to demand anything of God, but we can certainly request it, and He will move in His time and ways. When we demand things, or for God to appear to us so we can believe, He becomes a dispensing machine and nothing more.

Many wanted Jesus to do miracles for them. They told Him they would believe once He gave them a magic show. He didn't give them what they wanted. If you don't want to believe, and if you close off the ears and eyes of your heart, you won't see or hear Him, even if He's right in front of you. And if a miracle was performed before someone's physical eyes, it wouldn't move them if they didn't want to be moved. Doubt would remain, and there would always be greater demands for more. One's own volition is involved here. God says, "*I love those who love me; and those who diligently seek me will find me*" (Proverbs 8:17). He never promised to appear to give anyone a dog and pony show.

Submission is a verb, and it requires a willful heart. God can still hear the heart even when the mouth can't send out a prayer.

Lives Radically Changed

Although so many transformed lives convinced me of the truth that Jesus was who He said He was, this was the clincher for me: the changed lives of the disciples. The disciples and Jesus' brothers are additional evidence of life transformation. What moves cowards into a place of becoming brazen spiritual warriors, even to the position of martyrdom?

When Jesus was arrested in the Garden of Gethsemane, the disciples were around him, but they fled. They scattered and ran for their lives. The disciple John appeared at the crucifixion with Mary, Jesus' mother. All the other disciples ran for cover, hid, cowered, and in terror, locked themselves away so they wouldn't be found.

Then came the resurrection. Something radical happened to change these men from sniveling cowards to bold and shameless spiritual warriors for Christ. What was it? Jesus appeared to them in physical form, wounds and all. And as we know, after the resurrection, over five hundred people (1 Corinthians 15:3–8) witnessed Christ walk the earth for forty days before His ascension to Heaven. Many new believers gave their lives because of their transformation. Even Jesus' own half-brothers, who were doubters beforehand, came to believe He was the Messiah after the resurrection. They wouldn't relent or deny what they'd seen, and they wrote the books of James and Jude (which were their names) in the Bible. Each of them died a martyr's death.

All of the disciples, with the exception of John (who wrote the end-times book of Revelation) were martyred for their faith, but many newer believers also gave up their lives. Why? They wouldn't deny the reality of what they'd seen and experienced. The resurrected Christ walked the earth.

Would they die for a lie? People will die for a lie if they believe it to be the truth, such as radical zealots who believe they'll gain a great reward in the afterlife if they give their life for their faith. However, no one who knows that a lie is indeed a lie would be willing to die for it, let alone let their family die alongside them. If these witnesses knew Jesus' resurrection was a hoax, they wouldn't do such a thing at such an extravagant expense.

The Word and the living Word (Jesus) spread like wildfire, yet thousands of Christians died for their faith. In several countries today, they still do. The evidence of transformed lives, starting with the number of witnesses who saw Him alive after His resurrection, changed lives forever.

Other transformed lives give solid testimonies of Christ's power to change people.

John Newton grew up without any religious conviction and became involved in the Atlantic slave trade, bringing men and women from Africa to the coast of America. He shackled them while taking them overseas. Rape and death for these future slaves were all part of the travelling hazards.

One day, his sea vessel hit a violent storm, and he cried out to God for His mercy. After being saved from the storm, he continued slave trading but began studying Christian theology. Once he really knew Jesus, he grieved and mourned his part in the slave trade and was so moved by God's grace that he wrote the words to one of the most-loved Christian songs. Written in 1773, "Amazing Grace" is a much-loved hymn, even today. If God's grace can cover John Newton, God's amazing grace can cover any of us. There is no sin so great that the shadow of the cross cannot cover it.

David Wood was an atheist who believed that ants and animals were the actual beings that ruled the world. Listening to his testimony astounded me. I couldn't believe how God could transform such a life.

He grew up with a lack of feeling or emotion toward others. David tried to murder his father for no reason, just because. While in jail, he met a fellow inmate named Randy. Randy had an encounter with Christ, and once Randy became a Christian, he turned himself in to the authorities for his past felonies. David mocked and ridiculed him for his belief in the Bible, but Randy didn't back down. He challenged David with his own thinking process, asking him questions that he didn't want to think about or answer.

One time, Randy decided to do a forty-day fast, just as Jesus did. David thought he would outdo both Randy and Jesus by a day or two. David was in the habit of challenging himself to outdo another, and as Randy fasted and prayed, David was determined that he would beat Randy's fasting period. While trying to fast for such a long period of time, David became very sick and fainted. The guards, thinking he was trying to commit suicide, took him into a secure cell with cameras to monitor him. Once in his cell, with nothing to do and no one to converse with, he began taking Bible courses. He got straight As, which he felt was hilarious because he didn't believe any of it. His sole purpose was to come out of there with more ammunition to argue with Randy.

Being stuck in a solitary cell, he began studying the walls surrounding him. It was here that David's perception of his reality began to crumble. He could see the bricks were layered in a formation that would make the structure of the building. He thought that if someone told him that this structure of the bricks just happened by chance, he would think of them as an idiot. Yet there was such greater complexity outside of the brick walls. How could any of it be just chance?

This was the catalyst that caused him to begin his search and began changing his messed-up life. God took the rubble of this man's broken-apart world and in some miraculous way was able to construct something beautiful. His transformation began when he began applying biblical principles to his life. He went from being an atheist to a Christian apologist. Dr. David Wood has an incredible testimony of the dramatic change Christ made in his life and how Jesus turned his upside-down thinking and made it upside right.[25]

The platform where I gleaned David's story is no longer available, but there are many other incredible life transformations and testimonies for you to listen to on iamsecond.com. Each story is different and unique, just like the individual. Some of these people are well-known to the world, but God cares about each individual, whether they're known or not. We are well-known to Him, and that's what counts. We are equal in His sight and have great value and worth because of our Creator, not because of status or occupation. One may recognize some of the faces of famous people giving their testimonies on this site, but God recognizes the heart. We're already somebody just because we're His.

I can't fathom anything but a tectonic shift in the heart to change a mindset like David Wood's. Only God could perform such a miraculous work. When lacking faith in our prayers for others, we can hold on to these testimonies. We can see the power of prayer move through someone like Randy, the dedicated friend of David's, who prayed and fasted for the inmates and David himself. We can know that God hears and sees. Our almighty God moved in David's hardened heart. The power of prayer is powerful indeed!

---

*There is no sin so great that the shadow
of the cross cannot cover it.*

Part Three

THE FOREGROUND

Chapter Twelve

THE
CHURCH AGE

Since the disciples' time, believers who've accepted Jesus as their personal Lord are considered part of the "Church Age." This is the body of believers who know Jesus as Saviour and are labelled as the "Church." It's not a building but a body of believers. The "Church Age" started on the Day of Pentecost (Acts 2) and continues until the Rapture occurs. It began with the Jewish followers first, and once Peter had a revelation vision from God (Acts 10), it included the Gentiles. During that vision, Peter was told not to call anything unholy or unclean that God has cleansed and made holy, referring to the Gentiles, or non-Jews. The salvation plan was for all.

The Gentiles

After the vision, Peter was led to a Gentile named Cornelius (Acts 10). That vision did such a work in Peter that he would soon start preaching the good news to the Gentiles and not just the Jewish people. When Peter entered Cornelius' home, Cornelius fell at his feet and began worshipping him. Peter quickly responded and told him to get up, for "I too am just a man." This is a crucial point. Peter was a servant of God—simply a man and not to be worshipped.

I'll go on a bit of a rabbit trail here, but stick with me; I'll bring this back around—we are not called to worship people but God alone. So if a religious leader is demanding worship of any sort, or we're bowing to that leader as an idol, remember Peter in this situation.

When Thomas saw Jesus after the resurrection, he worshipped Christ, and Jesus did not stop him, because He is part of the Trinity.

God alone is the one to be worshipped; Jesus is God, so He is right-fully worshipped.

Not a person, or even an angel, should be worshipped (Colossians 2:18; Acts 10:25; Revelation 22:8–9). This is imperative because some religions began when an angel appeared to someone. Revelation 22:8b–9 gives us some significant information on worshipping angels. When John saw the angel, he tells us that:

> … I fell down to worship at the feet of the angel who showed me these things. And he said to me, "Do not do that; I am a fellow servant of yours and of your brothers the prophets, and of those who keep the words of this book. Worship God!"

Good to know—so we are not to worship angels! In case you happen to see one, and it appears to be an angel of light, don't let appearances fool you. I don't normally run into angels, but if one comes *your* way and wants to give you instructions, ask that angel who he serves, and that will give you the answer. An angel who is truly a messenger from God will not allow himself to be worshipped; instead, he will rebuke you the same way he did Peter: "Don't do that!"

If anyone has hooked up with a religion that started with angel worship, even angel card reading, these passages are worth remembering. Angels are messengers from God and used for God's purposes; they are missioned to point us to Him. Because most of us wouldn't be attracted to darkness, some angels appear as light. Both humans and angels are servants of the Almighty God and are not to be worshipped but instead used for His honour and glory. They are not God. If any angel demands worship, they are not angels of light. How do we know this? There was once an angel that demanded worship. He is known as Lucifer.

Now that was a bit of a detour, but it was needed and worthy of being read, not as a footnote but as part of the book. Now I'm off the rabbit trail and back on track. The Jews who were believers, as well as the Gentile followers, were known as Christians, or

114

"Christ-followers." They became one body, the "Church," but it took some navigating and deciphering, as you can well imagine. Much discussion was needed, and you can bet that circumcision was at the top of the list! There were two sets of ideas and cultures colliding yet somehow trying to come together as a body of believers. There were definite disagreements on things—blending strong Jewish religious tradition with the Gentiles, who were a mixed bag of nuts, was no easy task!

---

*Both humans and angels are servants of the
Almighty God and are not to be worshipped but
instead are used for His honor and glory.*

The Bride and Bridegroom

In the Church Age, the body of Christian believers are referred to as the "Bride." One body of believers who belong to Jesus, the "Bridegroom." Jesus refers to Himself as a groom in another story (Matthew 9:15; Mark 2:19–20), and God describes Himself as the "husband" of Israel in Isaiah 54:4–6, 62:4–5, and Hosea 2:19–20.

The parable of the ten virgins in Matthew 25:1–13 speaks about individuals as virgin-brides-to-be. Some of these virgins are prepared for their Bridegroom (Christ), and others are not. The other virgins don't have enough oil in their lamps, and when they go to get more, the Bridegroom comes and takes only those who are ready to go to the wedding celebration. Jesus gives us this parable. It parallels our preparation as the Bride (the Church of Christ-followers) and our readiness to be with Christ for eternity.

This parable refers to those who may think they're prepared to meet their Bridegroom, but they're not. These virgins must make a choice for themselves. Is Jesus the Bridegroom in their life? Are they prepared to meet Him? There are definite signs of a dedicated "virgin" ready for her Bridegroom. She eagerly awaits Him and is prepared no matter what hour He may come to receive her; she keeps herself pure for her husband-to-be and doesn't flirt with others; and she bears the fruit that comes with walking in purity. These examples parallel what the bride looks like according to the Jewish traditions and customs in Jesus' day.

The courtship described in this parable, the preparation to become married, and the marriage supper itself greatly resemble the Jewish tradition of courtship and marriage. After the bridegroom comes to get His bride, there's a wedding celebration. Christ comes to get His Church during the Rapture, and there are festivities with both Bride and Bridegroom in Heaven for seven years. On earth, however, this is the time of the seven-year Tribulation period. Yet even during the Tribulation, there is still hope for those on earth to accept Jesus as their personal Saviour. God gives humanity a second chance to come to Him.

When we know Jesus as our one and only Bridegroom, none of us need to fear the outcome of death. Death can come to any of us at any time, and we can be prepared. It's not death that needs to be feared but where we will spend eternity. In John 3:3b, Jesus tells us, *"Truly, truly I say to you, unless someone is born again he cannot see the kingdom of God."* That second birth, being "born again," is a spiritual one.

Falling Away

In the last days, the Bible tells us that a great apostasy will happen in the world. The word "apostasy" comes from the Greek word *apostasia* and refers to a "falling away." In 2 Thessalonians 2:1–4, Paul says that there will be a great "falling away" in the latter days, and we see precisely that. Our world has decayed and will continue to do so. We're falling away from God, churches are falling away from believing in the Bible as God's truth, and the world is falling away from God's moral code. Without God's moral code leading the world, morality will be a matter of personal choice, and the world will continue to crumble.

Presently, surveys show that over 50% of professing-to-be Christian churches do not believe in the inerrancy of Scripture.[26] We're told in 1 Timothy 4:1–2 and Matthew 24:11 that apostasy would occur before Christ came again. If one doesn't believe in the inerrancy of the Bible, then there is no moral compass. Everything swivels from the centre of that compass. Without belief in the Bible as God's total truth, who will judge what to dissect, keep in, or throw out? Who is righteous or wise enough to do so? The total Bible was meant to become our worldview, and those guidelines become an incredible plumbline to give us the best life possible (John 10:10). And sometimes that plumbline includes the tough stuff!

Today we have pastors and professors who no longer believe in God's Word as inerrant. And not believing that the Bible is the Holy and true Word of God will take us all over the map, causing churches, Christian universities, schools, colleges, and professors to offer students their personal beliefs rather than biblical teaching. One of my friends went to a Bible college, and her professor didn't believe in Heaven or Hell, even though Jesus talked about both. This is no longer rare, and teaching of this sort is happening at the top seminaries, Christian colleges, and universities. This type of education is causing waves of people who profess to be Christians to begin weaving their own doctrines, philosophies, and beliefs onto the canvas that God preserved for His Holy threading of Scripture.

When pastors don't believe that the Bible is God's whole and unadulterated words, we have wishy-washy Christianity. It's no wonder we have churches that don't teach us that the words from God are to be revered and that they're inerrant. Jesus tells us of such a church. On behalf of Jesus, the apostle John writes about seven churches in the book of Revelation. Each one received a message from Jesus, and each could represent any of our churches today. The church of Laodicea had become a watered-down version of Christianity. This church had a lukewarm faith flowing throughout the congregation. Jesus was firm: He would rather spit them out (Revelation 3:14–22) than see them remain as lukewarm believers.

With more than half of professing Christian churches teaching that they don't believe that the Bible is the accurate Word of God, we have apostasy—a falling away of the church. This type of teaching causes confusion among followers and mocks both the Bible and the Christian faith. Apostasy gets us comfortable with what we want to believe (and desire for self) as opposed to the truth of God's Word! But God knows the heart of His Bride, and they know Him and wait in purity for their Bridegroom.

What Is the Rapture of the Church?

This may surprise you, but the Bible teaches that physical death will not come to us all. There will be many who will not experience death. It's good to preface this subject by making the reader aware (if you don't know already) that there were a few individuals in biblical history who never died. Instead, they were "caught up" (raptured) in the heavens to meet God. Their names were Elijah (2 Kings 2:1–11) and Enoch (Genesis 5:21–23). They were righteous men, and their thirst for Heaven was greater than their thirst for the earth.

In 1 Thessalonians 4:13–18, Paul explains to the Thessalonians the mystery of "rapture." The root word is used in another passage where Paul is "caught up." It comes from the Koine Greek word *harpazo*, but in Latin it's *rapturo*, from which we get the word "rapture." In 2 Corinthians 12:1–4, Paul describes a rapture-like event in which mysteries were given to him by God, which he shares with the Thessalonians. He ends his discourse with encouragement: "*Therefore, comfort one another with these words*" (1 Thessalonians 4:18).

I believe that the rapture of the church, and the Tribulation period, are not allegories but literal events that will happen. I've seen the number of prophecies Jesus fulfilled during His first coming to earth. It's no longer a mystery as it was in the Old Testament era.

We now have the history of Christ behind us, and future prophecies before us, so I don't doubt that these future events will also take place.

After studying Jimmy Evans' *Tipping Point* online series and other lines of thought, I feel that the strongest evidence lines up with the rapture for the "Church" happening before the Tribulation period *and* also at the end of the Tribulation—right before or simultaneously with Christ's Second Coming. This will be a new idea for some Christians who think that they need to choose between the two, but there's enough evidence for both the pre-Tribulation and post-Tribulation Rapture.

Some educators on the subject seem to think that a Christian's rationale for hooking onto the pre-Tribulation Rapture idea is that they want to escape the seven-year Tribulation. They say that pre-Trib believers aren't preparing themselves for future hardship. I've studied both sides, and I maintain that we need to educate ourselves and strengthen our spiritual muscles to produce strong enough faith to go through whatever comes our way. There are personal tribulations in our own lives too, and it's a bumpy ride if we don't have spiritual stamina. No one can say with absolute certainty how the future will pan out. Both sides equally believe that they're correct and will tell you so with equal amounts of passion. Some things are simply mysteries that only God can weave into His timetable and in His way.

After much study, Evans changed his mind from his original viewpoint, that the Rapture would happen at the end of the Tribulation period alone. Based on Evans' forty-five plus years of study on the subject, he now believes two Raptures occur. Having two Raptures would clarify many questions. Believing in both a pre-Tribulation Rapture (before the seven-year Tribulation) *and* the post-Tribulation Rapture (after the seven-year Tribulation period) brings clarity to the debate. People think a choice needs to be made, but if there's a good rationale for both, there are also satisfactory reasons to believe that there could possibly be two Raptures.[27]

In John 14:1–3, Jesus tells His followers not to be troubled and that *"I am coming again and will take you to Myself ..."* (v. 3). In this passage and many others, Jesus tells us that He is coming back to earth, so we know He is arriving again. It's the Rapture timetable that's up for debate. In 1 Corinthians 15:51–53, Paul uncovers a mystery God revealed to him about the Rapture and shares it with the believers, who believe they missed the whole thing. He then reassures them that they did not miss it.

> *But we do not want you to be uninformed, brothers and sisters, about those who are asleep, so that you will not grieve as indeed the rest of mankind do, who have no hope. For if we believe that Jesus died and rose from the dead, so also God will bring with Him those who have fallen asleep through Jesus. For this we say to you by the word of the Lord, that we who are alive and remain until the coming of the Lord will not precede those who have fallen asleep. For the Lord Himself will descend from heaven with a shout, with the voice of the archangel and with the trumpet of God, and the dead in Christ will rise first. Then we who are alive, who remain, will be caught up together with them in the clouds to meet the Lord in the air, and so we shall always be with the Lord. Therefore, comfort one another with these words.*
>
> —1 Thessalonians 4:13–18

In this passage, those who are "asleep" are members of the Church who have died. These dead in Christ will rise first, and those still alive will be "caught up" with them. It's here where the Bride, the Church, meets her Bridegroom and is taken up into Heaven. The first Rapture is for the Church and happens before the seven-year Tribulation period begins. Other scriptures point out that the Rapture will occur before the Tribulation as well (1 Thessalonians 1:10, 5:9; Revelation 3:10). This is meant to bring us hope.

Believing in two Raptures will place the second Rapture at the end of the seven-year Tribulation period for those new and truly committed believers who perished during the Tribulation (Matthew 24:9; Revelation 20:4), giving up their lives for believing in Christ. They will now have eternal security. Then at the end of the Tribulation, Jesus comes in with His saints behind Him, and the whole world will see Him (Revelation 19:11–16).

Tribulation

Second Thessalonians 2 provides relevant information on this time called the Tribulation period. There is no allotted time mentioned in the Word between the Rapture and when the Tribulation starts. This could indicate that the Tribulation doesn't begin immediately after the Rapture. The world will be in such disarray and chaos after millions of people disappear all at once that we can assume this will be the catalyst that showcases the Antichrist. He then steps onto the scene and will be ushered centre-stage. He has a glow that appears to be saviour-like, and many will worship him, as the world will believe a "great lie" (Revelation 19 and 20). They will want hope and he will give it to them, but it's a false one.

With a Satanic force behind Him, He will achieve miracles of sorts and counterfeit the power of God with these performances. We have to remember that sorcerers from the past were spoken about and explained throughout the Bible, and they displayed powers as well, but they were limited. When Moses and Aaron were before Pharaoh, Aaron thew down his staff and it became a snake, but so did the sorcerers'. However, the staff of Aaron ate their staffs (Exodus 12:8–12). Pharaoh's sorcerers continued with other tactics, and at a certain point they could no longer go on.

During the Tribulation, the Antichrist performs counterfeit miracles (2 Thessalonians 2:9) and appears to have a Messiah-likeness about him, which helps to woo His audience. He gains power, and people worship him. His true colours will show when he demands to be worshipped. Remember the angel that rebuked Peter—only God is worthy of worship! If anyone doesn't do as they're told, he takes away their right to buy or sell (usher in the digital currency, where funds can be frozen). Another player on the scene, the false prophet, is his public relations person. Many eschatology (study of end times) teachers believe that this person will be a strong religious leader whom people trust, but he doesn't believe God's Word to be truth, and he convinces the world of their agenda.

There is a strong resemblance to the Trinity as well. The trio of Satan, Antichrist, and False Prophet mimic the Father, Son, and Holy Spirit, but only in a triangular formation. Jesus performed miracles of goodness and restoration in people's lives. He added and blessed. He never negated or took away. This may seem like an elementary principle, but it's one God deposited into my mind years ago: God is good, and the Devil is evil. God adds to our lives—add the "o" to God, and you get "good." The devil takes away from our lives—take away the "d," and you get "evil" (John 10:10). God gives, the devil takes.

Some who were not believers before the Tribulation period will then realize that Jesus is the only way to Heaven, and they won't take the mark of the Antichrist, a.k.a. the "beast" (Revelation 20:4–6). At that time, some new believers of Jesus may somehow escape taking the mark and manage to survive the worst part of human history, but I'm not sure what that could look like. Many believers will be martyred (Revelation 20:4–6). At the end of the Tribulation period, there will be a second Rapture for those "saints." Those who have placed their faith in Jesus during the Tribulation will be "caught up" and be a part of Jesus' homecoming, or second advent.

The Tribulation begins when a peace treaty is "confirmed" between Israel and the new world leader for one "week," meaning seven years (Daniel 9:27). It doesn't mention "signing" a treaty, so it's ambiguous. Whether it's a spoken treaty or a written one, this treaty marks the beginning of the Tribulation period. The Jewish people will be able to rebuild their temple for worship, if they haven't done so already (at the time of this writing, we have yet to see it begin being built). The end of the seven-year Tribulation period completes the 490-year prophetic calendar of Daniel discussed earlier in chapter nine of this book.

Three-and-a-half years at 360 days per year (according to the Jewish calendar) into the Tribulation (Daniel 9:27, 11:31–32), this leader will now demand worship from the Jewish people. He will come into their temple and fulfill the prophecy of the "abomination of desolation" spoken about in Daniel and by Jesus (Matthew 24:15–22). We are warned *not* to take the mark of this world leader, whatever it may be—a chip, tattoo, etc.—as that would mark us for him. Once that is done, it can't be undone, and then we have made our choice not to follow God or His salvation plan through Christ.

The Second Coming of Christ seems to happen simultaneously with the second Rapture. These saints who were martyred for their faith during the Tribulation, as well as any survivors who gave their lives to Christ—as many Jews will recognize Christ as their Messiah (Zechariah 12:10), and the Bride of Christ (first Rapture) follow behind Jesus for His second advent to earth. He cleans up the mess, and those who come against Him don't have a chance. Then He sets up His millennium reign on earth as King of kings and Lord of lords.

The Jews were looking for their King, and this will be Him! This will be the Warrior King they were looking for in Jesus' first coming to earth. It was never the Romans He was going to war against but Satan and his motley crew, those he rallied up to come against God and His Holy Word. The Isaiah 9:6 prophecy will be fulfilled, and the Child "born to us" will have the government resting on His shoulders, just as the reigning Messiah had promised. He will set up a literal millennium reign (one thousand years) on the earth (Revelation 20).

The prophecies, and therefore the evidence, of Jesus and His mission has been fulfilled once on earth when Jesus came, and it will be repeated again on His second arrival. There is knowledge to gain about the Tribulation, Christ's Millennium reign as King, as well as the New Heaven and the New Earth. I trust the authors I've recommended will help fill in the blanks if you desire to study these subjects further, and I hope you will pursue reading additional material to gain greater knowledge of future events.

Chapter Thirteen

THE
GENERATION

A number of Christ-followers who both study the Word and the prophecies of the future believe that we are the "generation" Jesus spoke of in Matthew 24. Jesus said that He didn't know the day or the hour of His second arrival but that we could know the generation of His return. The final generation Jesus spoke about isn't talking about *some* signs but about *every* sign that was foretold. There is an array of them that run through the Word.

Many scriptures foretell His return. Here are just a few: the signs in the heavens and other heavenly signs (blood moons and other signs), the falling away of a significant number of the churches that do not believe in biblical inerrancy (apostasy), the future Jewish temple that is getting ready to be built (every piece is now ready to be set into place), and God restoring the Jewish people to Israel (consistent moving of Jewish people back to the land since 1948). These events are described in Jimmy Evans' book *The Tipping Point*. Evans believes "that one generation will see all end times events fulfilled." That would include these signs being in the same period of time, or generation, of the Tribulation and the Second Coming of Christ.[28]

In Matthew 24, Jesus says that the generation that sees all these signs will be the one in which He returns. Since World War II, the final culmination of Israel's prophecies has been fulfilled. There are varying amounts of time given for a "generation" in the Bible, depending on the circumstance and God's will for each one. No one knows the hour or the day, but we can view the signs of the generation of His return. The markers are all around us. We can be aware and prepare.

Signs of the Times

The landmass of Israel is less than 1% of the world. It's approximately 290 miles long and 85 miles wide at the widest point. A landmass of this size should seem insignificant. Certainly the world shouldn't be centred on it. But this piece of land has become the epicentre for Bible prophecy—past, present, and future. It all happens here. There is a consistent stirring of controversy over this little piece of real estate, but I'm not surprised. God called it! If we know God's Word well enough, we see that end-time prophecy is magnified here. So where is most of the unrest in the world today? In and around Israel, exactly as God said it would be!

I'm only skimming the surface when I highlight a few of the signs. For a much broader view, I suggest reading material from the noted authors at the back of this book.[29] In the generation of Jesus' return, one obvious and strong sign centres on the Jewish people and the nation of Israel. Both the Jewish people and the land are referred to as "Israel" in some passages of the Bible, so in knowing that and when reading it, you can discern which is which.

The Jewish people have always been under persecution, and God has given them an unprecedented resiliency. Many cultures that should not have disappeared have vanished, but even though the Jews have been a tremendously persecuted people, their culture and language have not vanished. God has allowed them to flourish. We are reminded, *"For You have established for Yourself Your people Israel as Your own people forever, and You, Lord, have become their God"* (2 Samuel 7:24). Jeremiah 31:3b states, *"I have loved you with an everlasting love ..."* Furthermore, Jeremiah 31:35–47 gives insight into the depth of God's love toward Israel. His promises are true and forever.

Hatred toward any human being or people group is not from God. We can dislike or even hate one's sinful behaviour or deeds, but Christ died for all humanity, and His substitutionary death covered all sinners for all time. They still must choose Him for themselves, but He died for all. Hatred toward others and love for the cross cannot mix. Even when dying on the cross, Jesus looked upon those who crucified Him and asked the Father to forgive them, *"for they know not what they are doing"* (Luke 23:34). Maybe this verse is specifically given to us so we become aware that we are to forgive others, pray for them, and lay down that hatred at the foot of the cross, where Christ forgave His own trespassers.

Jesus, who is part of the Godhead, is Jewish, and the Bible, both Old and the New Testament, was written by Jewish people (there's some debate whether or not Luke was Jewish), who are God's chosen ones. In Romans 11:28b–29, Paul tells us exactly how God loves them: *"… but in relation to God's choice they are beloved on account of the fathers; for the gifts and the calling of God are irrevocable."* He is not finished His work with them yet. And God says His calling is *"irrevocable."*

Hatred toward others and love
for the cross cannot mix.

Grafted In

When the first print came out in August of 2023, there is no way that I could have known what was about to happen on October 7, 2023. We see a rise in anti-Semitism which is prophesied in the Bible. Zechariah 12:3 tells us that all "nations" will abandon their support of Israel. At the time of this writing, approximately one year after October 7, 2023, we see the United Nations doing exactly that. The imminent Gog and Magog war (Ezekiel 38 & 39) describes God defending Israel when all other nations abandon them. The idea of "replacement theology" is also spreading. This is the belief that the Christian Church replaces the Jewish people as God's chosen people and will receive His blessings. This theology has caused division among believers. Romans 11 tells us that the Gentiles are not replacing anyone; they're simply *"grafted in"* (Romans 11:17–24). Paul explains further that God is ready to graft the Jewish people (natural branches) back into their own olive tree anytime they're ready! Love, acceptance, and forgiveness— the fantastic attributes of a benevolent God!

We are called to love one another, and we're to look to the Bible for the answers of what that may look like. The good news of Christ's message of salvation was offered to the Jewish nation first and then presented to the Gentiles. Gentiles were grafted in, and they are offered God's blessing through that grafting. The Jewish Messiah and His salvation plan for the entire world made these gifts possible for everyone.

No takeover is needed; we can all be equally blessed because of Him. It doesn't have to be one or the other. That blessing is a free gift given to us through Jesus. God's love does not need to be rationed. When I became a parent, I wondered how I could possibly love my second child as much as the first. When the second one arrived, I couldn't fathom how that depth of love could become so deep, so quickly. And so it was with the third! That love was complete in an instant. I often think that God gives us reflections on earth of how it is in Heaven. God doesn't have to split His affection; He has enough love to go around and encompass His entire creation. How great is our God!

God is all-knowing, or omniscient. He knows the promises He has made, and He does not forget them. He is faithful to His Word, and His Word is truth. In Romans 11:18, we (Christians) are warned not to be arrogant about being grafted into the "branch" (the Jewish people and salvation through their Messiah): *"do not be arrogant toward the branches; but if you are arrogant, remember that it is not you who supports the root, but the root supports you."* Christians don't replace God's original branch just because we believe it to be so. His word is clear, and Romans 11 helps us to see that God hasn't changed His mind about His promises and fulfillment toward the Jewish nation: *"I say then, God has not rejected His people, has He? Far from it! ... God has not rejected His people whom He foreknew"* (Romans 11:1–2a).

In Romans 11, Paul explains why the Gentiles are grafted in, and he gives clear hope that the Jewish nation will one day—but not without significant and tremendous hardship—gain clarity about His future redemptive plans for Israel. Jesus will be recognized (Zechariah 12:10), and those redemption plans will come through their true Messiah. In 2 Samuel 7:23–24 and Jeremiah 31:35–37, we're reminded that God's Word is clear about His chosen people. His promises to the Jewish people and nation are irrevocable. He is forever their God. "Irrevocable" is a strong word, but God used it in this passage. There is enough bounty in our God to love His entire creation. How blessed we are!

Israel's Prophecies Fulfilled

In Matthew 24, Jesus prophesies to His disciples that the Jewish temple in Jerusalem during His day would be destroyed. A few decades later, it came to pass. The Romans destroyed the Jews' second temple in AD 70, along with greatly persecuting the Jewish people. When that took place, the Jewish people dispersed throughout the lands for about two thousand years, until now.

As they scattered, each adapted a different dialect of the Hebrew language mixed with their new country's native tongue. For example, Yiddish is a German dialect with Hebrew stirred in. There was no *one* common Hebrew language. After the Second World War, Israel became a nation again on May 14, 1948. Many Jews began trickling back to the land of Israel, and as they did, God reaffirmed His covenant with them. God's promises for this nation are outstanding, and they were all prophesied and fulfilled by God Himself.

In a little over a century, when they began tilling the land and planting trees, the number of prophecies fulfilled about the Jews and the land of Israel are outstanding. In fact, the Second Coming and His reign can't happen until these promises are fulfilled. Now that Israel has become a nation, all the prophecies are complete for this to become the generation of His return. I'll touch on a few of these prophecies: Israel becoming a nation in one day on May 14, 1948 (Isaiah 66:8); the re-gathering of the Jewish people to their homeland

(Isaiah 11:10–12); their desolate lands flourishing (Ezekiel 36:33–36); and making the biblical Hebrew dialect a language once again (Zephaniah 3:9). There are others. Israel is re-gathered twice as a nation, after the Babylonian captivity and in 1948 (Isaiah 11:10–12), and many Jewish people have returned from the North to their homeland (Jeremiah 16:14–15). Just over one million Jews immigrated from Russia alone between 1989 and 2002.[30]

All puzzle pieces have divinely been put into place. The pieces could not have been moved by human hands but only through the hand of God. One of the last building blocks for a future end-time forecast is the building of the Jewish temple. It needs to be completed by the middle of the Tribulation period, as it's where the "abomination of desolation" occurs, as referred to in an earlier chapter and in Daniel 9:27.

The Jewish people have been without a temple since the Romans destroyed the last one in AD 70. That temple was used to worship God and atone for their sins through the blood of animal sacrifice, as they did in the Old Testament. The New Testament changed the need for atonement through Jesus' death on the cross. In the Christian faith, we know that Jesus was the Passover Lamb that ended all sacrifices made at the Temple through His substitutionary and "atoning" for all the sins of humanity. But for the Jews who never recognized Jesus as their Messiah, they have a burning desire to rebuild their temple to worship God.

In Jerusalem, The Temple Institute has been working for years to have every single piece "ready-to-go" to rebuild their temple. From my last bit of research, everything is set to build in a moment's notice. The Jewish people desire to worship their Yahweh God in their temple once again. They have every instrument and piece of building material in place, right down to the training of the priests. It's a signpost and marker for the imminent return of Christ. The signs are here today. We don't have to look for any more clues.

Chapter Fourteen

THERE IS
AN ANSWER

There is an answer to our world's concerns. Jesus is it. But the world looks away! He has made Himself known, but only those who seek will find, and only those who search will discover. He is the Ancient of Days and the great I AM, as well as Lord and Saviour of the universe. The good news of the gospel of Jesus Christ is that we can come to know Him while we're still here on earth. Salvation is for all of humanity, but it's also personal and remains to be your decision.

We don't like to think about it, but we're all sinners (Isaiah 30:1; Romans 3:23; 1 John 1:8–10). The idea of sin tends to put us on the defensive because what may be a sin to me may not be a sin to you. The New Testament was written in Greek. Derived from the Greek word *harmatia*, sin is described as "missing the mark." Whose mark are we missing? God's mark!

If one fails to miss the centre of a target, they're off base and have missed the mark, and so it is with missing God's measure. He is perfect, and we are not. It's not about our interpretation of what sin may be. If we miss God's mark, that is sin. However, we will never be able to attain God's target of perfection because we're all sinners. That's where Christ comes in.

Christ Was Sinless

We are sinful, and Jesus was sinless. Second Corinthians 5:21 informs us that *"He made Him who knew no sin to be sin in our behalf, so that we might become the righteousness of God in Him."* He became the substitutionary spotless Lamb for the entire world to pay for humanity's sins.

In the Old Testament, the Jewish priests would sacrifice a spotless lamb (to represent purity) in the Jewish temple (Exodus 29:38–42) to atone for the sins of the Hebrew people. God also gave instructions for an annual Passover Feast as a memorial (Exodus 12:14). The Jewish Passover is a remembrance that every Jewish household sacrificed a lamb without defect at the time of the Jewish exodus from Egypt, which was led by Moses. They were instructed to place the lamb's blood over and on the side of their doorposts, and this would protect their household while the angel of death "passed over" these marked Jewish homes before they left Egypt.

The parallel between the two types of lambs (the animal and the reference to Jesus) and the instructions given for both are remarkably similar. Such as a spotless (sinless) lamb can have no broken bones (Jesus' legs were not broken on the cross), and the blood of the lamb needed to cover over death's door. (Jesus' blood covers us so that we can be in right standing before God.) Then, *exactly* on the day of Passover, Jesus was crucified and became the spotless Passover Lamb (John 1:29, 36) to take away humanity's sins forever. He gives us the freedom to accept or reject Him as the Lamb of God; through His blood over the doorpost of our heart, He delivers us (our exodus) and brings us from this earthly home to our heavenly one.

In 1 Peter 3:18, Peter explains, *"For Christ also suffered for sins once for all time, the just for the unjust, so that He might bring us to God, having been put to death in the flesh, but made alive in the spirit."* Jesus died once for all, and no more sacrifices are needed. Through His substitutionary atonement, we are put in right standing before our Holy God when we accept Him as our personal Lord.

It's not about what you have or have not done but what Christ alone has done for you. I like to call this the Great Exchange—His suffering for your eternal freedom. That is some gift! God's grace has been described as unearned merit. Ephesians 2:8–9 explains, *"For by grace you have been saved through faith; and this is not of yourselves, it is the gift of God; not a result of works, so that no one may boast."* A "gift" reveals to us that it's nothing we do; we just receive it (Romans 6:23). It is through faith alone.

Derived from the Greek word harmatia,
sin is described as "missing the mark."
Whose mark are we missing? God's mark!

God Is Holy

Isaiah 6:3 states, "*Holy, Holy, Holy, is the Lord of the armies. The whole earth is full of His glory.*" When entering God's presence, we also need to be sin-free. Jesus died in substitution for us, and His covering of righteousness gives us the passageway to enter God's presence with praise and thanksgiving (Hebrews 4:16). Jesus made a way.

John 3:16 says, "*For God so loved the world, that He gave His only Son, so that everyone who believes in Him will not perish, but have eternal life.*" Forgiveness through Christ came with a price and included Him dying for every horrific sin and ugly deed ever committed by every human being. He paid the price for the entire world, but not all choose Him or the works that He did on their behalf.

This offer of forgiveness isn't about our good works but His pure works. If it were about our good works and tipping the weigh scales of more good than bad, Christ would never have had to come to earth. However, even though He died for every sin and every person, it still comes down to our personal choice and acceptance of Him.

We need to both believe *and* receive. Many will believe in the historicity of Christ, and many will continue to go to church because it makes them feel better. There is yet another step one needs to take outside of believing, and that's receiving Him into your life and heart. John 1:12 tells us, "*But as many as received Him, to them He gave the right to become children of God, to those who believe in His name.*"

Christ Jesus' death on the cross has already paid for our sins. However, even though the payment has been made, like any paycheque, one still has to choose to collect it and deposit it for the transaction to be complete. You can come to Christ at any time and confess your sins and be forgiven right up to your point of death, but it has to be a willing and conscious decision you make for yourself. No one's prayers will save you afterward. There is no rewind button once you're dead.

Today it seems like the word "repent" is repulsive, but it's a word God uses throughout the Bible, and it's precisely what is required to make us accountable to Him. We willingly acknowledge our sin, confess, ask for forgiveness, and ask for His help because we know we can't change on our own strength or through sheer willpower or determination. There is a difference between godly sorrow and worldly sorrow. A godly sorrow mourns the sin and wants God to change the heart, which leads to repentance and salvation. Worldly sorrow may cause some pain, but often it's related to being caught rather than desiring to change (2 Corinthians 7:10). Repentance has been described as going one way and then making a conscious change to begin heading in the opposite direction. We used to walk away from God, and now we walk toward Him.

We Need a Helper

The Holy Spirit is God. Many names are given to the Holy Spirit, such as Author of Scripture (2 Peter 1:21; 2 Timothy 3:16), Comforter, Counsellor, Advocate (Isaiah 11:2; John 15:26, 16:7), Guide (John 16:13), Convictor of Sin (John 16:7–11), Intercessor (Romans 8:26); Indweller of Believers (Romans 8:9–11), and many more. Each one of these names denotes a specific attribute and role where He can be included in our lives if we invite Him in.

To keep things concise, I'll stick to one title—the Helper (Holy Spirit). When Christ left this earth, He said the "Helper" (John 14:26) would be here to assist us along the way. My goodness, do we need His help! This is the Holy Spirit's role in the Trinity. In this personal relationship, you can talk with Him like a friend. Psalm 139:7 asks, *"Where can I go from your Spirit? Or where can I flee from your presence?"*

He is omnipresent—everywhere at all times. You are not alone. In the process of our struggles, we can have help.

There's a vast difference between saying we are Christians and living life for self. If Jesus really is our Saviour and Lord, our lives will reflect it. Even if we struggle with sin, we continue to ask the Helper to come alongside and assist us to change. He can read the hearts of each of us. Even though we may struggle with certain habits or attitudes because of our fallen human nature, we rise up and confess, get in right standing before God, and ask for the Holy Spirit to help us. Then we partner with Him and start a new day. Committed faith follows with action. I call this spiritual integrity. We need to know the Word of God well enough to recognize where we need correction and direction so that our actions line up with our faith walk. Once we become a beacon for Him, we can be a light to the world. We are meant to mirror and reflect Jesus to others.

First Steps

Making things right with God is not about us but about Jesus. Many people think that they need to clean themselves up before accepting Jesus into their life. Not one of us would ever be ready in that case. You don't need a shower before you take a bath, and you don't have to clean yourself up before coming to Jesus. Come as you are. He will begin the work from the inside out. He paid the price. I love the words in Ezekiel 36:26: "*Moreover, I will give you a new heart and put a new spirit within you; and I will remove the heart of stone from your flesh and give you a heart of flesh.*" God can make a heart of stone pliable if we're willing to give it to Him. Nothing is impossible for Him!

Forgiving those who have hurt you is one of the first steps to becoming free from the bondage of hatred. Forgiving is more than just a thought and it's done. Forgiveness is an ongoing task. You can begin by saying it out loud, even if you don't mean it, because there is power in your tongue to change your heart. Proverbs 18:21a puts it this way: "*Death and life are in the power of the tongue.*" God can take a heart of stone and make it a heart of flesh. The key is that one must be willing.

Forgiveness is a journey. Speak out the name of the person you need to forgive so that you can get it out into the spiritual realm. Remember the Helper. You can give Him the authority to do that work in you. "I forgive (name)" releases the Holy Spirit to do the work you can't do. Asking God to give you a heart of forgiveness for that person invites the Helper on your journey of forgiveness. It's a process, but speaking it out is the first step to healing.

Forgiveness doesn't necessarily mean reconciliation. Some individuals have been deeply wounded and abused. Christ would never ask us to go back for more abuse. But it does depend on you and the Lord, because every circumstance is different. Forgiveness releases the hold that has gripped us and offers life and energy back to our lives. Withholding forgiveness imprisons us, not them. Remember, you are not alone on this path. You have the Helper.

Accepting Jesus Christ as your Saviour and Lord isn't a difficult step, but it's one that requires laying our pride at the foot of the cross. Our works reflect our love for Jesus, but they don't save us. Ephesians 2:8–9 says, *"For by grace we have been saved through faith; and this is not of yourselves, it is the gift of God; not a result of works, so that no one may boast."* God knows the sincerity of our hearts. Your life was meant to reflect your love for Him.

Once this is done, let me encourage you to begin rooting yourself in the Word of God. As well, attend a physical (but for some it may be online) church that believes that the Bible is God's total and only Word. A parable in the Bible talks about a sower (Matthew 13) who throws good seed on soil, but it's taken away. Be aware that the enemy does not want you to get started in your new faith, but when you get the right source of nourishment, your roots will grow. The journey of faith begins with germination—good seed being planted in your heart. It takes root but can easily be pulled out if we're not diligent.

When nurtured properly, it begins rooting deeper and develops into a vigorous plant that bears fruit. Growth is a steady and daily process.

Accepting Christ as your Saviour and Lord begins with a simple prayer. Even if you doubt, just confess it and pray anyway. He can work with that because He knows you. Be sincere with God. He knows what you're struggling with. I started at a place of doubt too but built my faith on the foundation of earnest seeking *despite* my doubt.

A simple prayer is all that is needed. The authenticity of your prayer will be between you and God. Genuine prayer will cause good seed to begin rooting in one's heart. We're not to wait. The Bible proclaims that today is the day of salvation (2 Corinthians 6:2). It is such a simple act but the most profound one you will ever make. The prayer goes like this:

> *God, I give you my heart and my life, each part of it, the good and the bad. I recognize that I am a sinner in need of You as my Saviour. Thank you that Christ died for my sins, was buried, and rose again on my behalf, which assures me of eternal life. Today I accept Jesus as my Lord and Saviour.*

There is nothing more powerful than the name of Jesus. He wants to work in you and through you. This genuine prayer has the power to transform your life and heart.

Hygiene Habits

Psalm 139:23–24 says, "*Search me, God, and know my heart; put me to the test and know my anxious thoughts; and see if there is any hurtful way in me, and lead me in the everlasting way.*" When we invite Jesus into our lives, a shift in the conscience begins to point us to a truth that guides our life. We have to do our part, beginning with spiritual hygiene habits. This can take place in a variety of ways. We read and study the Word of God, pray, memorize scripture, choose awesome worship music, ask for the Holy Spirit's guidance and help, fellowship with other believers, and attend church to help us grow, learn, and continue on our journey.

During the COVID-19 restrictions and isolation, I probed myself to think about what I took for granted—going to the movies and restaurants, seeing people, and worshipping at church. One question I asked was: What if our freedom of worship is taken away? We have to think of that because it could be a strong possibility. On and off throughout COVID, our places of worship were closed and then open for a short time. It went back and forth with changing restrictions. However, churches may not always be open, or we may not always be able to speak the Word of God freely and without penalty.

Cancel culture has started to move in and aggressively push out God and His Word. We can't rely on the government or any other source for our faith. It's up to each of us to grow, learn, and memorize scripture so that we have God in our hearts and lives. If the doors of our churches close, we still need to be able to nourish ourselves spiritually. We cannot or should not rely on the government. The government will not recognize Jesus, and many will continue to mock Him, just as they did in His day. So nourishing ourselves spiritually and having good hygiene habits is a personal responsibility.

Chapter Fifteen

FOREVER
HOPE

Our hope is in Christ alone! He is the true Messiah, and if we die today, tomorrow, or years from now, our eternal destiny can be secured. The fact that you're here in this period of history and reading this book is evidence of a God who wants you to know Him and be aware of upcoming future events. The hope we have secures our future with an eternal destiny.

The Bible describes the Messiah as a suffering Servant who takes away the sins of the world during his first advent on earth, and as a reigning King after His second advent. On His first visit, He came to serve as the sacrificial Passover Lamb who died on the cross for the sins of humanity; at the second advent, He comes as a Warrior King with His children behind Him (Revelation 19). He wages war against the Antichrist, the false prophet, Satan, and the enemies of God (those who follow the Antichrist). The battle is not ours, but His.

The Invite

In Revelations 3:20, Jesus says, *"Behold, I stand at the door and knock; if anyone hears My voice and opens the door, I will come in to him and will dine with him, and he with Me."* This was one of the first verses I learned as a young Christian. It was a personal invite, and I accepted it. It wasn't a forced entry. I love this verse. I saw a picture of this piece of scripture in a bookstore I often visited when I first became a Christian. I'd study this picture of Jesus standing at the door and knocking, with the verse below it. One day, someone pointed something out to me that I had never noticed before. On the outside, where He stood, there was no door handle. Jesus could only enter if someone opened the door and invited Him in. He stands at your door and knocks today. It is an invite. He will not force Himself in.

Mark Twain once published a book called *The Prince and the Pauper*. Although Twain's book was not about one individual's dual role, I wrote this story to remind me of Jesus's role on earth.

He came to earth concealed as a pauper, and as a true prince will one day be King. He took on a humble appearance and left His throne to be with His people, to be like them, live among them, and become a servant for them. Eventually He would die for them. It was a deliberate act of love. Then He would rise from the dead to become the future King and do battle with the enemies of God. His kingdom would be an eternal one, and although the entire kingdom was invited, not all chose to follow Him. His eternal dwelling place was offered to everyone through His atoning death and was for all humankind throughout the land. However, many took roads that led them elsewhere. Their desires led them on trails to distant lands that, in the end, were barren. They didn't want to study who He truly was, even though He made Himself known and stood before each of them. There was time and opportunity on the earth to observe, but they looked away. They chose not to see that this pauper was indeed the prince, and the prince would one day be the King. He was simply concealed beneath the cloak of a humble Servant. In the end, those who recognized Him, loved Him, and desired to be with Him would become the children of the King. One day, His inheritance would be their inheritance too.

For those who want to open their eyes, they will see; for those who want to hear the good news, they will hear. It is the greatest mystery the world has ever known! The most amazing paradox we could imagine! Under the humble cloak He once wore, He actually wore a robe of righteousness. He served the world as a pauper and one day will serve as King. He came meek and mild as a Lamb and will rule someday as the Lion from the tribe of Judah. He is the King of kings and Lord of lords. He is the Author and Finisher of our faith. He is the light in a dark world. He adds salt to a tasteless life. He is spiritual Bread for the hungry and Living Water to those who are spiritually thirsty. He came humbly the first time, and He will come triumphantly the second time. He is the Alpha and Omega, the Beginning and the End, the Ancient of Days. He is our Rock, our Strength, our Anchor, our Fortress, our Friend, our Lord, our Saviour, and our God. In Him alone we will find security, safety, and an eternal dwelling place of peace.

He is the certainty in uncertain times.

BIBLIOGRAPHY

Alcorn, Randy. *Heaven*. Carol, IL: Tyndale Publishers Inc., 2004.

Ankerberg, John and Wheldon, John. *The Facts on the Mormon Church*. Eugene, OR: Harvest House, 1991.

Arndt, Tim. "6 Undeniable Ways Jesus Changed the World for the Better." Allendale Baptist Church. Accessed February 23, 2023. https://allendalebaptist.org/jesus-better-world.

Behold the Man—A Journey into History Seeking the Real Jesus. DVD. 2006; Worcester, PA: Vision Video.

Canadian Bible Society. *the poverty and justice bible*. Swindon, UK: The British and Foreign Bible Society, 2008.

Eareckson Tada, Joni. *Heaven: Your Real Home*. Grand Rapids, MI: Zondervan, 1995.

Evans, Jimmy. *Tipping Point: The End is Here*. Dallas, TX: X.O. Publishing, 2020.

Geisler, Norman. "Has the Bible been Accurately Copied Down Through the Centuries?" SES, August 21, 2017, https://ses.edu/has-the-bible-been-accurately-copied-down-through-the-centuries/.

Graham, Franklin. *Living Beyond Borders*. Nashville, TN: Thoman Nelson, Inc. Publishers, 1998.

Hampson, Todd. *The Non-Prophet's Guide to the Book of Revelation*. Eugene, Or.: Harvest House, 2019.

Lewis, C.S. *Mere Christianity*. New York, NY: HarperCollins Publishing, 1980.

McDowell, Josh. *The New Evidence That Demands a Verdict.* San Bernardino, CA: Here's Life Publishers. Inc. 1999.

Milne, Bruce. *The Message of Heaven and Hell.* Downers Grove, IL: Intervarsity, 2002.

Ova, Johnny. "The Roman Guard Evidence for Resurrection." Sound of Heaven Church, April 28, 2020. https://www.soh.church/the-roman-guard-evidence-for-the-resurrection/.

Stoner, Peter W. *Science Speaks.* Chicago, IL: Moody Press, 1963.

Strobel, Lee. *Case For Christ.* Grand Rapids, MI, Zondervan, 2016.

Tsarfati, Amir. *Israel and the Church.* Eugene, OR: Harvest House Publishing, 2021.

Whiten, Russ. "HAVE YOU EVER WONDERED: Is the Bible Historically Accurate?" THE DESTIN LOG, June 15, 2017.

https://www.thedestinlog.com/story/lifestyle/faith/2017/06/15/have-you-wondered-is-bible-historically-accurate/985681007/.

Wood, David. "David Wood: From Nihilism to New Life." Premier Christianity, April 14, 2016, https://www.premierchristianity.com/home/david-wood-from-nihilism-to-new-life/2666.article.

ENDNOTES

Chapter Four

1   Randy Alcorn, *Heaven* (Carol, IL: Tyndale Publishers Inc., 2004), 361.

Chapter Five

2   Tim Arndt, "6 Undeniable Ways Jesus Changed the World for the Better," Allendale Baptist Church, accessed February 23, 2023, https://allendalebaptist.org/jesus-better-world.

3   Canadian Bible Society, *the poverty and justice bible* (Swindon, UK: The British and Foreign Bible Society, 2008), back cover.

4   Franklin Graham, *Living Beyond Borders* (Nashville, TN: Thoman Nelson, Inc. Publishers, 1998), 105.

5   Phillip Schaff, *Quotes by Philip Schaff*, Goodreads, accessed February 23, 2023, https://www.goodreads.com/quotes/8345526-jesus-of-nazareth-without-money-and-arms-conquered-more-millions.

6   *Behold the Man—A Journey into History Seeking the Real Jesus* (2006; Worcester, PA: Vision Video), DVD.

7   H.G. Wells, *HG Wells Quotes About Jesus*, AZ Quotes, accessed February 23, 2023, https://www.azquotes.com/author/15487-H_G_Wells/tag/jesus.

Chapter Seven

8   C.S. Lewis, *Mere Christianity* (New York, NY: HarperCollins Publishing, 1980), 52.

9   Randy Alcorn, *Heaven* (Carol, IL: Tyndale Publishers Inc., 2004), 285.

10 Bruce Milne, *The Message of Heaven and Hell* (Downers Grove, IL: Intervarsity, 2002), 194.

11 Joni Eareckson Tada, *Heaven: Your Real Home* (Grand Rapids, MI: Zondervan, 1995), 53.

Chapter Eight

12 Josh McDowell, *The New Evidence That Demands a Verdict* (San Bernardino, CA: Here's Life Publishers. Inc. 1999) 202.

13 Johnny Ova, "The Roman Guard Evidence for Resurrection," Sound of Heaven Church, April 28, 2020, https://www.soh.church/the-roman-guard-evidence-for-the-resurrection/.

14 Russ Whiten "HAVE YOU EVER WONDERED: Is the Bible Historically Accurate?" THE DESTIN LOG, June 15, 2017, https://www.thedestinlog.com/story/lifestyle/faith/2017/06/15/have-you-wondered-is-bible-historically-accurate/985681007/.

15 "Is the Bible Reliable?" *Got Questions*, accessed February 23, 2023, https://www.gotquestions.org/Bible-reliable.html.

16 Norman Geisler, "Has the Bible been Accurately Copied Down Through the Centuries?" SES, August 21, 2017), https://ses.edu/has-the-bible-been-accurately-copied-down-through-the-centuries/.

17 "How does Archeology support the Bible?" *Got Questions*, accessed August 6, 2024, https://www.gotquestions.org/archaeology-Bible.html.

18 Lee Strobel, *Case For Christ* (Grand Rapids, MI, Zondervan, 2016), 159.

19 John Ankerberg and John Wheldon, *The Facts on the Mormon Church* (Eugene, OR: Harvest House, 1991), 30.

Chapter Nine

20 Todd Hampson, *The Non-Prophet's Guide to the Book of Revelation*, (Eugene, Or.: Harvest House, 2019), 19, 68.

21 "Does the Bible Mention Alexander the Great?" Got Questions, accessed February 23, 2023, https://www.gotquestions.org/Alexander-the-Great.html.

22 Hampson, 28.

23 Peter W. Stoner, *Science Speaks* (Chicago, IL: Moody Press, 1963).

24 Josh McDowell, *The New Evidence That Demands a Verdict* (San Bernardino, CA: Here's Life Publishers, Inc., 1999), 195–201; see also "What Are the Seventy Weeks of Daniel?" *Got Questions*, accessed March 17, 2023; see also *My Search for Messiah*, 2006, United States, Day of Discovery; see also "Old Testament Prophecy: Royal-Decree," Jewish Roots, accessed March 22, 2023, http://www.jewishroots.net/library/prophecy/daniel/daniel-9-24-27/royal-decree.html.

Chapter Eleven

25 David Wood, "David Wood: From Nihilism to New Life." Premier Christianity, April 14, 2016, https://www.premierchristianity.com/home/david-wood-from-nihilism-to-new-life/2666.article.

Chapter Twelve

26 "Signs of Decline & Hope Among Key Metrics of Faith," Barna, March 4, 2020, https://www.barna.com/research/changing-state-of-the-church/.

27 Jimmy Evans, *Tipping Point: The End is Here* (Dallas, TX: X.O. Publishing, 2020), 221, 222.

Chapter Thirteen

28 Jimmy Evans, *Tipping Point: The End is Here* (Dallas, TX: X.O. Publishing, 2020), 217.

29 Amir Tsarfati, *Israel and the Church* (Eugene, OR: Harvest House
    Publishing, 2021); see also Todd Hampson, *The Non-Proph-
    et's Guide to the Book of Revelation* (Eugene, Or.: Harvest House,
    2019); see also Jimmy Evans, *Tipping Point: The End is Here* (Dal-
    las, TX: X.O. Publishing, 2020), 217.

30 Jan Markell, "When Dry Bones Come to Life" YouTube,
    September 10, 2021, 58:32, https://www.youtube.com/
    watch?v=dmJAgoroMPo; see also Our Daily Bread, "Signs of
    the End Times," YouTube, May 22, 2020, 24:50, https://www.
    youtube.com/watch?v=VC_JMPLkJRE.

www.ingramcontent.com/pod-product-compliance
Lightning Source LLC
LaVergne TN
LVHW051100080426
835508LV00019B/1985